I0151239

IN PURSUIT OF LIBERTY

Notes of an Immigrant

Zinovy Gutman

In Pursuit of Liberty: Notes of an Immigrant
Zinovy Gutman

This book is a memoir. It reflects the author's
present recollections of events and experiences
over time. Some names, characteristics, dialogues,
dates, and sequences of events may have been
recreated.

ISBN: 978-0-578-45528-0
Library of Congress Control Number: 2019901074

Cover design by David Ter-Avanesyan
Edited by Deirdre Stoelzle

Table of Contents

Prologue

The idea for writing down this story came to me from the questions my wife and I often hear in casual conversations from people who learn that we immigrated to the United States from the Soviet Union almost thirty years ago. How did it happen? Why did you guys decide to go? Did you just wake up one morning, look at your wife and say, "Honey, let's pack up the kids, we are moving to America"? And of course, the famous "Do you like it here?" even after thirty years in the country.

Telling our story in simple terms of a few sentences always leaves it incomplete, missing something, leaving out something very important. The desire to finally tell it fully and completely is the reason for this book.

Looking back on those years, we now realize that whatever happened to us there, in the Soviet Union, was not only about us. Our decisions were driven by a chain of historic events and omens preceding the collapse of the huge empire we lived in at that time. The real true rationales behind our decisions are woven into the background details of those historic events.

1

To show that background, I must touch on several attributes of life in the Soviet Union at that time—social, political, economic, even religious, to some extent. Most of it will be in the first couple chapters, so please bear with me while I set up the scene.

The stories described in this book are essentially notes of an eyewitness, real experiences, facts and episodes we either participated in or have been an eyewitness to. To separate the narration of these events from my subjective thoughts and analyses, I am using "Notes" printed in italics for my thoughts, analyses, and some additional information.

A note. I have always believed that we, the people who physically moved to the United States and became American citizens, are the first-generation Americans. Just recently, in a casual family conversation, my children explained to me that the first-generation Americans are my grandchildren who were born here.

"Then who are you?" I asked.

"We, who came here as kids, are the immigrants," my children responded.

"Well, then who are we, your mother and I, who brought you here?"

"You," my children shrugged their shoulders, "can probably qualify as pilgrims."

So, my reader, let's submerge into the brine of the Union of Soviet Socialist Republics in the second half of the last century and try to figure out why the pilgrims would leave the place they were born, the place they grew up and lived for eight or more generations, and decide to board the metaphorical ship to lands unknown.

The Melikha

Everything depends on a point of view. Looking at an asshole from the inside may seem like a light at the end of the tunnel.
(Old Soviet wisdom.)

At the time I was born and raised, according to the official Soviet gradation, the country was experiencing the period of the developed socialism. I can say this with a certain level of expertise since I studied all this nonsense as a mandatory discipline in my technical college. During the first year students studied the history of the Communist Party of the Soviet Union; the second year, Marxist-Leninist philosophy; the third year, political economy; and the fourth year, principles of scientific Communism. The well-known secret was that neither the professors, nor their students, and not even the authors of the curriculum textbooks, had a clear understanding of the content of those subjects, especially the last two. Just think about it for a second. How can the word "political" help a struggling economy? And what can make Communism "scientific"? But the Melikha made us study it and we studied.

A linguistic note. Melikha is a Yiddish word, derived from the Hebrew מַלְכוּת which can be translated as a kingdom. But, as with many other Yiddish words, it has a slightly derogatory and ironic flavor and was used in certain areas of Ukraine, with a dense enough Jewish population, to describe the Soviet ruling regime, having the meaning of "the kingdom in trouble."

Initially, as we were taught in school, the country was supposed to build Communism, with the slogan "From everyone according to his ability, to everyone according to his needs." However, at some time in the past, the Communist Party realized that, because of those damned American imperialists and Zionists, they did not have enough goods to give to everyone according to their needs and switched to a socialism model with a slogan "From everyone according to his abilities, to everyone according to his contribution." I do not recall receiving a clear explanation of what differentiates "developed socialism" from just regular socialism. My guess is that this was a hidden message to us, the people, from the ruling Melikha that this is "as good as it gets" and "don't count on it getting any better" because it had been already fully developed.

The same slogan, if you think about it, can be applied to the market economy. Those who work to the best of their mental and physical ability are

5

evaluated by the market and are rewarded according to their contribution. The determining factor differentiating between the two economic models becomes who is evaluating the contribution? In the socialist model this task is assigned to the corrupt bureaucracy; in the market model the evaluator is a collective behavior of members of the society, the market. Obviously, the market is a much fairer and more objective evaluator than the corrupt Melikha and is, because of its collective nature, a better match for a democratic society.

Comparing the market and socialist economic models is like comparing the operation of a large and complex system in fine-tuned automatic mode and operation of that same system in manual mode, pardon my engineering analogy. Add to this analogy that the ruling bureaucratic elite, who are operating the system, are not necessarily composed of the brightest representatives of the society. In the automatic mode they probably could have maintained the system with more or less success, but in manual mode their operation turned into disaster.

The Soviet planned socialist economic system constantly faced two challenges: controlling the production and controlling the distribution. The production part presented very little interest to the general population; everyone just laughed when the government would announce their customary "the highest achievements ever recorded in history." The unfair distribution, however, annoyed populaces a lot. The Kremlin geniuses could plan anything they wanted on the production side, but nobody wanted to work without the rewards. As a result, the productivity in the socialist economic model was very low and there were less and less goods produced for the distribution. With perpetual deficits, most of the distribution was happening between the ruling elites, leaving the rest of the population with just enough to prevent them from hunger riots. If the scourge of the market economy is overproduction, the scourge of the planned socialist economy was underproduction.

As far as I remember, there was always scarcity of everything—food, clothing, shoes, furniture, you name it. The scarcity of goods created enormous corruption and universal, comprehensive theft. And as years went by, it got worse and worse. Since there was no private property and everything supposedly belonging to all, taking what you could became a morally acceptable societal norm. In the words of a famous Soviet comedian Mikhail Zwanetsky, "you have what you guard," meaning that a chef has free food, a forest ranger has free wood, and so on . . .

An observational note. At any of the government, industrial, or commercial facilities in the United States, the security checkpoints are always at the entrance to the facility, exits are never guarded.

The Americans just want to make sure that you are authorized to enter the facility. In the Soviet Union it was to the contrary, the security checkpoints were always at the exit, the authorities wanted to make sure that the visitor or the employee did not steal anything.

The worst situation in the socialist Soviet Union, however, was always with the distribution of housing. The private housing sector did theoretically exist but was very limited after the expropriations in the '20s, especially in big cities like Kiev, where I grew up. There was a very limited and heavily regulated co-op sector. To become a member of a cooperative took an overwhelming amount of money and very strong connections. The majority of us lived in government-owned apartments similar to the American projects. The apartments were distributed at the place of work. The waiting lists were humongous, a person could wait all their life working at the same place and never move up on the waiting list. Several generations could end up living in a small, 25-30 square meters (270-325 square feet) apartment and consider themselves lucky that their father got that unit twenty or thirty years ago. Can you even imagine the level of bribery and corruption in the process of distribution of those apartments? Finally, there were still the communal apartments, meaning a three to four room apartment occupied by three to four families. Each family occupied a room and shared the kitchen and the toilet with the neighbors. Both my wife and I spent our early childhoods in such communal apartments, we still remember. I forgot to mention that many people also lived in the dorms. If a government enterprise, an agriculture machinery manufacturing factory, for example, needed additional workers, they would build a dorm for housing those workers with a promise to put them on a waiting list for a future apartment. People would move in, usually from the countryside, get married and have children who would grow up in the dorms, go to school from the dorms, and still wait for their turn on the waiting list. I was on a business trip around the year 1987 in the Ukrainian city of Nizhyn and saw those families with my own eyes when I stayed in such a dorm for a few days.

A side note for those who still believe in socialism. The great-sounding idea just does not work in practice. Not because "the Russians did not do it right." Many nations tried this model on all continents around the globe from Europe to Asia, from Africa to Latin America. It did not work anywhere. The best argument that I ever heard against the socialist model came from my professor of economics at Cal State East Bay where I was taking my MBA classes. Originally from Romania, the professor was very passionate about the subject. "Look at Germany," he told us. After WWII, the country was artificially divided into west and east parts. By circumstances, not even by their choices, West Germany took on a market economic model and East Germany took on a planned socialist economic model. They were the same people, known to the world for their great ingenuity and work ethics. The same culture, the same language, the same pre-conditions — a perfect scientific experiment! The division lasted slightly more than 40 years, enough to see the results. West Germany produced BMWs and Mercedeses, automobiles renowned for their quality and luxury. East Germany produced STASI, secret police renowned for its brutality.

Every time, anywhere in the world where the socialist model was tried, it led to poverty, endless wars, ruined millions of lives, and produced ZERO results.

There were multiple other nuances within the Soviet system that made the horrible housing situation even worse. One of them was the mandatory permanent-residence registration. It meant that everyone's address or permanent residence, as it was called, was written in ink in everyone's passport and could only be changed if a person obtained permanent residence in another place. Doing this was almost impossible due to previously mentioned waiting-list lines. The exception was marriage. By registering the residence of its population, the Melikha achieved its goal of controlling the movement of this population, but at the same time foolishly restricted that movement, hence restricting the economic growth.

The Fifth Line

Every Soviet citizen had a nationality written down in their birth certificate and passport. The birth certificate had two lines for nationality—mother's nationality and father's nationality. At the age of 16, when the passport was issued, a person inherited the nationality of their parents. If the parents were not of the same nationality, the person could choose either their mother's or father's nationality. Other choices were not allowed. The person's first name was written in the first line of the passport, the father's name in the second line, the last name in the third, date of birth in the fourth, and the nationality in the fifth. This made a phrase "the fifth line" infamous for "troubling" nationalities.

Judaism in the Soviet Union was not a religion, it was a nationality. In my case, for example, I was born in Ukraine, my ancestors lived in Ukraine I'd guess for at least three to four centuries, I was fluent in both Ukrainian and Russian languages, and walked, talked, and behaved exactly as my Ukrainian counterparts. But I was not a Ukrainian, I was a Jew because that is what was written in my birth certificate and passport.

11

A nationality note. Please understand me correctly, in no way I am complaining or regretting that I was born to my Jewish mother and father. To the contrary, I am thanking Providence for this gift every day of my life. The purpose of this chapter is to explain to my reader that the socialist society was not a free society the way it was trying to portray itself. There was no freedom of religion, no freedom of movement, no freedom of choice. It was rather a modern form of subjugation, where the individual's destiny was pretty much pre-determined by the circumstances of his or her birth.

The Melikha divided its population into the nationality groups and controlled those groups at will. Some were getting preferential treatment, the Melikha's version of affirmative action, others were punished. The Jews were punished.

One more nationality note. Not only the Jews were punished. During my years in college in Tula, Russia, I met some German guys. Their ancestors moved to Russia at the time of the Russian tsar Peter the Great at the beginning of the 18th century. Just like me, they looked like Russians, they talked like Russians, and they acted like Russians. I am not even sure they knew the German language beyond what they learned at school. But, their fifth line was marked "German" and they had their own problems with the Melikha as "Germans."

As far as I can remember from my early childhood, being a Jew never gave me any warm feeling or comfort. Jewish community as such did not exist, synagogues did not exist, there was no information at all about what it meant to be Jewish, no religion, no history, nothing. Silence at best. The surrounding environment was hostile, the family was trying to hide it as much as possible, especially after the WWII genocide. The boys were not even circumcised out of fear to be identifiable, because this method of identification was widely used by Nazis and the Ukrainian nationalists collaborating with them. This is how they would pick Jews out of a lineup to kill. During my early childhood years our family lived on Nagornaya Street in Kiev, right above the Babi Yar where tens of thousands of Jewish people were exterminated, and I remember my mother sometimes quietly crying looking out the window. I did not understand why but could feel it was somehow related. Negativity without explanation. When meeting a fellow Jewish kid in kindergarten or elementary school, we pretended to not acknowledge each other because, honestly, we did not know what united us other than the hostile environment. The revolution, civil war, Stalin's repressions, and World War II on the top, wiped out our identity almost completely. Neither my parents' generation, born in the '20s, nor mine knew much about our religion, history, or culture. A few words in Yiddish here and there did not count. Sometimes I am amazed how our parents had the courage to have children under those circumstances. Judaism as a religion practically did not exist. Four millenniums of our history were wiped out.

Another note about religion. All religions in the Soviet Union were suppressed, not just Judaism. Even Orthodox Christianity was very limited and under complete control of the KGB. I remember one of my coworkers in the late '70s in Kiev decided to baptize his baby daughter. The next morning, he was called to the human resources department to explain himself in front of the former KGB officer who customarily ran those departments.

So, no Hebrew schools, no Christian schools, Bibles were not printed for a half century, atheistic and communist propaganda with hefty chunks of antisemitism taught from kindergarten through college, newspapers, radio, and TV pushing propaganda in full force. Jews were completely deprived of their history. When we studied History of Ancient World in fifth grade, the Kingdom of Israel was not even mentioned. According to the Soviet version of ancient history, it did not exist. The Egyptian civilization was immediately followed by the Greek civilization. Jews were not considered to be a nation and were often called in the newspapers "the kinless cosmopolitans." By cutting access to any information, they almost convinced even us. All that was left for our self-identification was our famous fifth line.

A note. Funny how our Jewish history allows our adversaries to define and distinguish us when we fail to do so ourselves. The same fifth line in our passports and birth certificates that was our hardship in Soviet Union, gave us the opportunity to emigrate in the '90s. Jewish rabbis in Israel consider these Soviet-era documents to be legitimate proof of being a Halacha Jew. Similar story happened to the European Jewry. After WWII when the State of Israel was establishing itself, Israelis had to decide who from the European survivors should have the right of return to Israel. Since Nazis were considering a quarter of Jewish blood enough to send a person to the concentration camps, Israelis decided that the same quarter of Jewish blood should be enough for the right of return.

The ignorance and national depression, at least in my case, lasted up to 1967, when I was eleven years old. That year the "Israeli aggressors finally exhausted the patience of freedom-loving Arab people and a just wrath of Arab anger crashed down on the aggressors' heads." With sinking hearts, we were watching the news, children and adults alike, showing us how "the liberating Arab armies were marching and approaching evil Tel Aviv to resolve the Jewish problem once and for all." Then suddenly . . .

Silence! One day, second day . . . nothing, no news, like nothing ever happened. And we knew in our hearts what the silence meant. I started seeing cautious smiles on my parents' faces and on the faces of my Jewish neighbors. Little by little, by word of mouth, from jammed shortwave radios, from other unknown sources, we started to learn that yes, the Jews actually won that war in 1967, that somewhere far, far away there is a Jewish state and there is a Jewish army, and we are not kinless, and we are not alone. For me, for people I knew, and I am sure many others, that was the beginning of our Jewish national awakening. I remember getting together with the other Jewish kids during the recess at school and whispering about the news from out there. For many of us it was the first time we felt an urge to communicate with each other about "that" subject, and for the first time the feeling was warm and positive. I cannot say that in the year 1967 we suddenly learned more about ourselves than we knew in the year 1966, but awareness was certainly aroused.

Everyone in my generation probably went his or her own way in search of self-identify. I received mine from an absolutely unexpected source, the Christian Bible. Around 1974-1975 when I was in college and was already dating Tatyana, my future wife, her mother traveled back to their native Yaroslavl deep in Russia for a funeral of an old family friend who happened to be a religious lady (very rare case at those times). When she came back, she brought back with her that lady's old Bible. This book had a big cross on the cover and was issued before the revolution in archaic Russian language. I saw the book lying on a shelf, presenting no interest to anyone in their family. To them it was nothing more than a sentimental item from the late Grandma Shura, or Baba Shura as they called her.

At about that time I was studying Marxist philosophy in my college and had to prepare a report on atheism. The college was purely technical, but the subject was mandatory. On those kinds of subjects, like religion or Western philosophic theories, the approach we were taught to take was a strong rejection and denial without any explanation or "G-d forbid" additional information. But I, already having been instructed on how to study technical disciplines, decided to look at the source and asked Tatyana's mother's permission to look into the book from Baba Shura. The book turned out to be the Old Testament. How surprised was I to find out in the third chapter that Avraham was a Jew! It was written black on white that "Then there came the fugitive and told Avraham, the Hebrew . . . " Wow, then apparently all the other patriarchs in the previous and the following chapters were also Jewish, and G-d, whose existence I was supposed to question in my report, is the Jewish G-d, and the whole book is about us, and I am not kinless after all!? Of course, I read the book to the last page and of course I did not mention any of it in my report. The shock was enormous! I shared everything I read with Tatyana. She was the only person around whom I could trust. When I came home for the summer break, I told my mother what I learned and was surprised by the fact that she already knew a little bit about the subject. An even bigger surprise was how little she knew. I was trying to talk to my friends, Jewish and not Jewish, those whom I could trust, but nobody seemed to care. So, I continued to live with this knowledge, hidden inside. I have to say that James Orwell in his book *1984* described the psyche of an isolated, thinking individual inside the totalitarian environment pretty accurately. I did not become religious; the religious aspect did not touch me that much. It was rather another stage in my self-awakening, the realization of belonging. A huge chunk of missing information suddenly fell into place, I became more informed, capable of own independent analysis, and armed against the propaganda.

Years later, here in America, I read Golda Meir's memoirs, in which she describes her visit to a Moscow synagogue on the eve of Rosh Hashanah in 1948. She was the Israeli ambassador at the time and a crowd of about 50,000 came over just to see her. No speeches, no actions, no greetings, people just stood around her, touching her dress and crying. I was not there, I was not even born yet, but when I read about it, I understood their feelings. Another story I heard was about The Barry Sisters' visit to the Soviet Union in 1959. Posed as an American folklore band, they blasted the hall when they started singing their songs in Yiddish! Most of the audience happened to be Jewish, because who else in Moscow would go to a concert of American folklore music? I was not there, but I can only imagine.

Looking back at my early years, I cannot say that in the '60s and '70s there were all-out persecutions, nighttime arrests, or public trials like there were in the '30s and '50s. The country was going through the Khrushchev thaw and then through Brezhnev's indifference. Nobody believed in anything anymore and nobody cared. Unless you acted or said something that may threaten their power, the Melikha would leave you alone. But the message to us Jews was very clear—there is not enough for everyone, so Jews should not even bother to apply. There was a well-known anecdote circulating in the '70s. The story went that there was a rumor circulating through town that tomorrow in one of the stores there would be smoked salmon for sale. Early the next morning, at sunrise, a huge line running for several blocks was already formed in the freezing cold. At the time of the store opening, the store manager came out to the crowd and announced that there would not be enough fish for everyone, therefore the Jews would not be served and may leave the line. All the Jews sighed and left the queue, other people got a little more excited and closed the ranks. After about four or five hours of waiting in the cold, the store manager came out again and announced that he just received a phone call from the District Party Committee, and that because of some unexpected problems with supply, there would be less fish than they originally expected and only the Communist Party members would be served. Well, people got upset, but left the queue. Only the party members remained in the much shorter line. After another couple of hours, the manager came out and announced that there would only be a very limited amount of fish delivered, therefore only the members of the Communist Party who participated in the 1917 revolution would be served. At this point, only a half a dozen very old men stood in the freezing cold for another couple of hours until the store manager finally invited them inside. He took them into his office, sat them down, offered them tea, and then confidentially explained the difficulties in the international situation and the crafty plots of the imperialistic enemy, and told them that as old party members they should understand that there would be no smoked salmon sold today at all. Everyone sighed again, stood up and started moving toward the exit. Suddenly one of the old men turned to the manager: "Listen," he said, "I can understand the international situation and I can understand the difficulties with supply . . . but why should those Jews always have privileges?"

The folk wisdom, as always, got it right. In addition to the overall hardship of survival for everyone inside the Soviet reality, the Jews were forcefully pushed to the side. This was a simple bone that the Melikha could offer to the populace at a low cost to itself, and the populace did indulge it. It's always pleasant to see someone worse off than you are.

Therefore, the only method of survival available to us was trying "to be a little better to be equal." Work a little harder, study a little more diligently, get an education. Education was a goal in every Jewish family I knew. Some succeeded, some did not, but everyone tried.

An almost-positive note. All I describe above is my personal comprehension of the situation of the Jewish people in the Soviet Union in the '60s and '70s of the last century that was digested with my later life experiences and looked through the prism of living in a free society for the last almost thirty years. Back then we did not have enough information to do any analysis. We hated the situation, but had to accept it the way it was, we had no other choice. People surrounding us, our environment, accepted the situation the same way, as it was. We grew up in Kiev all together— Ukrainians, Russians, Jews, and whoever else happened to be around. We went to the same school, played soccer in the same courtyard, chased the same girls, and fought with the kids from the neighboring city block. We were all friends and remained friends for many years, even after we came back home from our colleges or military services and became adults. I am still in contact with some of my Ukrainian friends. Those were the guys I could trust. With them I could sit around the kitchen table and discuss political events after a couple shots of vodka, and not be afraid to be arrested the next morning. That was worth a lot in those days! But it is a pity to admit that everyone, including even those closest friends, accepted that treatment of us as a given, as a justifiable norm. I can only hang the blame for this on the Melikha, as another crime committed, this time, against its own people.

Education

Education in the Soviet Union was free, kind of what our homegrown American socialists are now proposing, from first grade to a doctorate in the top university. Everyone was entitled to college education, they just needed to pass the entry exam. Doesn't that sound nice? Sounds nice until you hit the reality of having something in limited supply for free. As soon as the market is taken out of the equation, corruption immediately takes its place and the entry exam becomes the tool for manipulation. The exam to enter a technical college consisted of four parts: an oral exam in math, an oral exam in physics, a written exam in math, and a written essay in Russian. There was no multiple choice, you had to answer the given questions. Exams were not anonymous to the examiners, the name of the examinee was written on the top. Test results for the oral exams were given on the spot, results for the written exams were announced a few days later by posting a printed list of participants and their grades on the doors of the office. Gradation was a five-point system with 5 being excellent; 4, good; 3, satisfactory; and 2, unsatisfactory. Results could not be disputed. At the end, theoretically, all enrollees who passed all the tests with at least a satisfactory grade were ranged and the top of the list, matching the number of enrollment positions, were accepted. Theoretically . . . First of all, the children of the elite were guaranteed acceptance. The higher the rank of the elite parents, the more prestigious colleges would be accessible for their child.

A quick note. This is why I had the audacity to say earlier that the elite were not composed of the brightest representatives of the society. They simply did not have to go through the natural selection.

Second, remember the corruption? Third, there was a certain quota for some special groups of the population, kind of like American affirmative action. In Russia there were quotas for certain minorities, in more monogenic Ukraine the special quotas were reserved for remote country regions versus cities. I do not have data to confirm my statement, because during the Soviet era these statistics were a top secret, but at the same time they were well known to everyone. So, all the suckers with their great grades were competing for the few leftovers. But wait! Remember the fifth line in the passport? In Ukraine, Jews should not even bother to apply because the quota for this particular minority was zero. By the way, the quota for Jews in the tsar's Russia was 3%. Anyone still want to participate in the revolution?

I am not writing this paragraph to complain. This was just an objective reality we lived in during those years, the reality that later was probably one of the major factors that led us to emigration. Would anyone who reads this book want to put their children through this experience? The statistics I can use to prove my point are simple: Out of all Jewish guys and gals I knew in my age group, my schoolmates, those a few classes above and below my grade, my friends, my relatives, and so on, only two Jews were accepted to college in Ukraine. It was Kiev Pedagogical Institute, not a very popular college because it did not have a military department (I will explain later) and the teachers' salary was minuscule. I would estimate that the density of the Jewish population in the area where my family lived was about 20%. So, I am talking about a sample of close to a thousand people. Two out of all of them. Remember, education was free to everyone.

A note. Practically all Jewish youth pursuing education had to go to the remote regions of Russia where there was a low density of Jewish population and we were not assigned to a special category, hence had a chance to be accepted.

Neither of my parents received a higher education. My father graduated from a secondary technical school and was working as a construction manager. My mother, as far as I know, made it to the Pedagogical Institute, but dropped out when she married my father, and later worked as an accountant. My older sister attended a secondary medical school and became a pharmacist. My parents dreamed of a higher education for me, especially my father who, from working in his trade, understood the value of it.

I wanted to follow my father's footsteps and become a civil engineer. My grades at school were good, but not great, and parents hired private tutors for me. So, on the weekends, instead of having fun and playing soccer with my friends, I had to take the bus to the other side of the city and swot up damned physics and math. Well, this was the only way to "be a little better to be equal."

A note. My reader may ask me where could we find tutors, if private businesses were not allowed? The answer is simple: The market is immortal. If it becomes suppressed, it goes underground and becomes a "black market."

When the time came for me to fill out my college application, my father went to his old Ukrainian friend whom he knew from the construction business and who at the time happened to work at the Kiev Auto Transport

Institute. My father asked him if he could find out from the college administration what my chances were for being accepted there. The response from the college administration was honest. If this man is really your friend, they said, tell him not to waste his kid's time, the chances are zero. My father was very disappointed, this was his only hope.

At this point in my story I have to explain the military factor. In the Soviet Union every male at the age of 18 was liable for a military call-up. If a person was accepted to college, the draft was postponed until after graduation. Universities and technical colleges had military departments. Study in a college lasted five years. Starting from the second year, all male students attended military departments one day a week for four years until the graduation. During this time, they were trained as reserve officers in a military specialty close to their civilian study. Dropouts were immediately drafted. Right after civilian graduation, all male graduates were sent to military camps for three months for the oath-taking, field practices and the final exam. Those who passed the final exam (practically everyone did) were granted a lieutenant rank and sent into the reserves. A few were enlisted as needed, sometimes even voluntarily. The students of the nontechnical colleges that did not have military departments, like the Pedagogical Institute, for example, were allowed to graduate and then were drafted as soldiers.

So, military service was unavoidable. I personally never burned with desire to be in the military, but if I had to serve, I'd rather serve as an officer, at least they were better fed.

Most of us were graduating school around seventeen. School had 10 grades, elementary, middle, and high school all under the same roof. We entered school at seven and graduated at seventeen. School from first to the eighth grade was mandatory. After eighth grade a person could either go to work, apply to a secondary or trade school, or continue for the last two years in high school. College applications were accepted in June, exams in July and August. I was lucky to be born in mid-August. I graduated high school before seventeen, and potentially had two chances to apply to college before the military draft at eighteen. Those who were born earlier were doomed to only one chance. As you can see, in our beautiful Union of Soviet Socialist Republics, the concept of "fair" did not exist, it was what it was, and everyone had to live with it.

Losing all hope of studying in Kiev, my family decided that my only chance was to leave Ukraine and go to Russia. There was a common belief among the Jewish population that in Russia, except Moscow and Leningrad, there was less antisemitism than in Ukraine. But where to go? Russia was a huge red spot on the map to the east

28

of us. My father started thinking of any relatives he had in Russia, but there was none. Then he remembered about his childhood friend Mikhail Torpusman, Uncle Misha to me, who visited us several times when I was a small child, I barely remembered him.

A linguistic note. It was customary in Russia and Ukraine for children to call their non-related family friends "aunt" and "uncle." This was a matter of showing respect to the elder rather than defining the level of blood relation.

After the war, Uncle Misha graduated from a secondary mining school and was assigned to work in the mines in the region of Tula. He picked a very unusual and dangerous trade and joined the mine rescue team. When there was an explosion, or a fire, or a collapse in the coal mine, while everyone else was trying to run out, he and his guys were trying to get in and rescue the survivors. During the time I am talking about, Uncle Misha was a commander of the Mining Rescue Detachment. So, my father wrote him a letter asking him if he knew of someone who could check to see if I would have any chance sending my application to the Tula Polytechnical Institute. To our surprise the response came very soon. Uncle Misha happened to have a friend in the Mining Department and that friend told him that yes, if I pass all tests with decent grades, I may be accepted. Perfect, this is all we were asking for, to at least give us a chance. So, Tula Mining Department it was.

After that, Mama started crying and I cannot blame her because I was not even seventeen yet, very small and skinny. My height as an adult is 5'-5", back then I was obviously even shorter. The argument that won her over was that if I did not go to Tula then, I would be drafted in a year anyways and, though it did not stop Mama from crying, the deal was set. If you ask me, I personally did not mind going somewhere new and sent my application to the Tula Polytechnical Institute's Mining Department without any doubts. Since I wanted to be a civil engineer, I chose the specialty of Construction of the Underground Facilities and Mines. As I found out later, I could have probably applied to the Civil Engineering Department and still have been accepted with my grades, but who knew back then?

A few explanatory notes to my American readers. First, the schools of higher learning in the Soviet Union were divided into institutes and universities. Not sure how exactly they were distinguished, I guess the universities had more departments and may have done some research. My alma mater Tula Polytechnical Institute a few years after my graduation became Tula State University without any visible changes, so go figure. The second note is that in the Soviet educational system there was no practice of selecting classes. The application and then the enrollment was for a certain pre-selected engineering specialty. Upon being accepted, each student was assigned to a group and was taking the pre-determined set of disciplines with this group, following the pre-determined schedule. Of course, for the general education classes several groups could have been assembled into a larger auditorium, but you still had to take your class with your group on certain days and at a certain time.

Tula

A few words about Tula. Tula is a relatively big industrial city in Russia situated approximately 200km (120mi) south of Moscow with population at that time of about 500,000 people. Tradition says that when Russian tsar Peter the Great found out that the region had deposits of coal and iron ore in close proximity to each other, he ordered the creation of armory shops in that area and build the city of Tula. Truth or not, the armory factories are still there, along with coal- and ore-mining operations. Another distinguishing characteristic of Tula is that it is located roughly 200 kilometers from Moscow. By Russian rules, both tsars' and modern, released prisoners, both criminal and political, can settle no closer than 200 kilometers from Moscow, the infamous 201st kilometer rule. This, of course, gave a distinguishing flavor to the city's population.

As you could've already guessed, I passed the tests with decent enough grades and was accepted to Tula Polytechnical Institute. I got 4 in oral physics, 5 in oral math, 5 in written math, and 3 in Russian essay. It was more than enough to pass. Apparently, in Tula Jewish enrollees were not singled out as special group, but were assigned to the "others" category, which allowed me to blend in with the crowd and, therefore, be accepted. I was a little disappointed with my essay grade because I knew that I could write essays and my grades at school were much higher. I could feel that there was no anti-Semitic prejudice in my marginal grade, but I just could not figure out what went wrong. Later on, I got it.

There were two reasons for the low grade on my Russian essay. First, Ukraine, and especially Kiev, was even then a bit of a runaway province with tendencies of looking toward the West with a more independent way of thinking than in a mainland Russia. Our high school Russian Literature teacher, Clara Sergeevna, encouraged us to show our personal originality, unique thinking, and non-standard approach in our essays, even within the limits of the standard, full-of-propaganda school program. In my essay I tried to do just that, which was a big mistake in more conservative Tula.

Secondly, as my new Russian friends explained to me soon after I arrived, the language I spoke was not classical Russian. Though Russian was the primary language in Kiev, it was peppered with Ukrainian, Yiddish, and Polish phrases and idioms, which in my opinion made it more colorful than the classical Russian spoken in Tula. Some of this flavor could have slipped into my essay and probably was not appreciated by the local experts.

A linguistic note. Being very young and receptive, I quickly started picking up the local Tula dialect. But when I would come back home for breaks, my mother would tell me to stop messing around and speak normally. Ever since, every language I speak has some sort of an accent. Here at home in the U.S. for example, while communicating with my wife we have gone even further and use all the languages we've picked up along our way, often simultaneously.

College classes always started on the first day of September. I came to Tula by train, transiting in Moscow, at the end of August of 1973 to study Underground Construction. I was directed to the Mining Department dormitory and settled there. The dorm was a four-story, U-shaped brick building with two shared restrooms per floor in the wings and two shared kitchens per floor in the central stretch. Four students were living in each room. The beds were military-style with a spring net and cotton mattress plus a cotton pillow and a wool blanket. Everyone got a nightstand next to the bed and one shared wardrobe per room. There was a radio on the wall. The beddings were exchanged twice a month. On an announced day you had to take your dirty set downstairs to a special room and exchange it for the fresh set. If you missed the date, too bad, you must wait till the next one. There was one "normally closed" shower on the first floor. If my memory serves me right, it worked maybe a couple times in the few years I spent there. There was no laundry.

Practically everyone in the dorm was living in the little miners' towns around the city and went home every weekend. That is where they took their showers and gave their dirty clothes to their mamas to wash. My mama was too far, and I realized very quickly that I had to somehow resolve this situation. I found a public bathhouse at the other end of the city near the railroad station and was going there to take my showers and wash my clothes by hand every weekend for years. It was only about half an hour each way on a public bus. The fun part was coming back in the winter, in the freezing Russian cold. Oh, yah, there was a big notice posted up at the entrance of the bathhouse saying that doing laundry was prohibited. Well, this was another one of Melikha's rules that I regularly broke because laundromats or any other way of washing clothing just did not exist.

The payment for the dorm was very small, if I remember correctly only 15 or 20 rubles for the entire year. Every student at the Mining Department with passing grades received a stipend of 50 rubles a month. Straight "5" students were getting a heightened stipend of 65 rubles. My last two years in the college, when I hit a heightened stipend, I was making more money than my wife, who was already working as a librarian for 62.5 rubles a month.

Students from the same groups were usually placed in the same rooms. So, upon arrival, I acquainted myself with my new roommates, who were also about to start studying Construction of Underground Facilities and Mines.

On the first day of school I was summoned to the Mining Department office and was informed that I could not continue studying Construction of Underground Facilities and Mines. My visual acuity did not satisfy the admission requirements for the underground works and my only remaining option was to study Opencast Mining. That put an end to my civil engineering career and started my mining engineer career.

To this day I cannot understand what happened. Every one of us had a physical checkup before our applications were even accepted. The Mining Department knew very well about my farsightedness way ahead of time. Whether it was human error or that someone's baby needed to take my place at the last moment, I do not know.

The department's secretary gave me my new schedule and the next morning I joined my new group. Luckily the guys from Opencast Mining were living in the same dorm next door. I remained in my original room till the end of the school year and now I had bodies in both groups.

After two weeks of study all students were summoned to work at the collective farm for about a month. Autumn was the season for gathering potato crops and the country needed our help. It was another genius invention of the Kremlin "wise" men. Instead of admitting Stalin's mistake with collectivization and giving the land back to the farmers, they were using students and military as the agricultural workers. No wonder there was always a shortage of food in the country.

A side note. I keep showing these examples of a complete failure of the socialist economic model because I can see the tendencies in the modern American mindsets, especially among the youth. The leftist elite and academia are glorifying the socialist model as being an acceptable alternative for creating a just and prosperous society, manipulating the idealistic and often naive minds by giving them half the truth. One of the U.S. senators, who openly proclaimed himself a "socialist,". visited the U.S.S.R. in his youth. He should have seen what was going on there . . . If he saw and continues to promote socialism for his political gains, he is not honest. If he was there and could not see it (if the Melikha was able to pull a veil over his eyes), he must not be very smart. This is my cry in the wilderness, my humanitarian duty, if you wish, to tell you what I've seen. We lived through this mess, ask anyone who came from a socialist country—Poland, Romania, Bulgaria—they will all tell you the same. If you want to see shortages of potatoes in Idaho, go ahead and try socialism!

So, the studies were interrupted, the groups were loaded into buses and delivered to different collective farms. The last two kilometers of the journey to our collective farm we rod a sledge pulled by a tractor, there was so much mud that the buses could not get through. Our setup was not bad. We were living in the big, empty, two-room house, probably twenty of us, not sure whom this house belonged to. The collective farm was providing us raw food — meat, milk, potatoes, grains, and bread. We set up rotation shifts of two guys staying home to cook and clean, while the rest would work all day in the field. For the collective farm the labor was practically free. I believe at the end, when we returned to Tula, everyone received a few rubles. The collective farm apparently paid us some sort of minimum wages for the farm work, deducting the cost of food and transportation, and then dividing the remaining money equally between the group. The good news was that this month was a good bonding experience, it built a comradeship between us, really formed the group. In those circumstances it was easy to see who was who and who was worth what. Most of the group was of my age, 17 to 18 years old, but there were probably four or five guys who enrolled after serving in the military. Of course, they were the elders and were calling all the shots.

There was a convenience store in the village, belonging to the collective farm, and a post office. I was able to send home a couple letters.

Sunday was our day off. Our best entertainment was catching pigeons and frying them on the bonfire. To be precise, we caught them the night before. Next to our place there was an old church building that had been turned into a warehouse. Pigeons were sleeping in the attic, all happy and fat, living off the neighboring threshing-floor grains. If you snuck up on them at night with a flashlight, they would not even try to fly away, and you could just grab them and put them into a sack. I did not even know before this that pigeons were edible, not to mention the hunting techniques, but of course took part in the operations. My excuse to the pigeon-rights activists is that we were hungry.

One of the guys had a camera and took a picture of me in my high boots and a warm quilted cotton jacket. When we came back to the city, he developed the photo and gave it to me. I thought I looked so good in this photo, so grown-up that I decided to send it home to my mother with a letter, overlooking the fact that I was holding a lit cigarette. My poor Mama, I had a lot of explaining to do when I came home for break.

One day I got sick with some kind of a cold. I barely made it home from the field and fell into the bed. The guys realized that something was wrong with me and found a thermometer somewhere in the village. My temperature was above 40C (104F). After a brief discussion, the elders pulled together some money, went to the store and bought a bottle of vodka. They carefully poured a glass, generously added black pepper, and gave it to me to drink. The rest of the bottle was split between the elders and quickly disappeared. I cannot say that I was so innocent that I had not had vodka before, but not in such amounts and certainly not under such circumstances. After I drank my glass, they moved my bed next to the fireplace and I do not remember anything else that night. Next morning, I woke up all sweaty and very weak, but with normal temperature. I was freed from my duties that day, served in the kitchen the next day, and was back to the field on day three all happy and healthy like a young bull.

When we returned to Tula, sometime at the end of October of 1973, my real student life began. My biggest challenge was finding something to eat. There was nothing like an American college campus with food courts. Remember that private businesses were prohibited in the Soviet Union and that included restaurants. Therefore, even the concept of fast food did not exist. The situation with slow food was not much better. There was a cafeteria in the neighboring dorm, run by the government, of course. The menu was simple—

cream of wheat for breakfast, soup and schnitzel with pasta for lunch, and the same schnitzel for dinner. The quality of food was questionable; I already mentioned in the beginning the ubiquitous theft that people were forced to commit throughout the country. The women from that cafeteria had to feed their families from whatever supplies the cafeteria was receiving. The ingredients on our plates were whatever was left over. So, after about a week, that schnitzel was no longer a palatable option. There was very little variety of food in the stores. Bread, some questionable cans, margarine, maybe sugar, flower, salt, and pepper. Much worse than in Kiev. But one way or another I found my way around. My parents were sending me 30 rubles every month, and combined with 50 rubles of my stipend, it was enough for a modest student living.

The best time in the dorm was Sunday evening. That's when roommates in the dorm were coming back from home, bringing with them food, most of it in the form of raw ingredients. Everything was shared, and we immediately rushed to the kitchen to claim a gas-stove burner. The challenge was that nobody really knew how to cook. After a few tryouts I was designated as the cook; my soups and fried potato were at least edible. My secret was that as a young boy my Jewish mama made me do my school homework in the kitchen in her presence, because otherwise

I would easily lose my concentration. So, I dug into my memory and tried to reproduce her cooking sequences. It worked! You never know what info can be useful at some point in your life.

It was not a one-way street, of course. When I would come back from breaks, I always brought stuff with me and the food my parents could buy for me in Kiev was a treat to my Tula roommates. Plus, my parents would send me food parcels once in a while and of course I shared it all with everyone.

Communication with home was either through letters or sporadic phone calls. My parents in Kiev did not have a landline phone, not everyone did. Phone communication was through the post office. If my parents wanted to talk to me, they would go to the post office in Kiev that had a long-distance phone service and order the call, usually for Sunday. The post office would then send a telegram to my dorm that I had a phone call ordered from Kiev on Sunday at a certain time. I would show up to the central post office in Tula, the only post office that had a long-distance phone service, notify the receptionist lady that I had arrived and sit in the waiting area. Then there would be an announcement, "Kiev, third booth." I'd run to the booth, pick up the phone, and talk to my parents. This was a pretty expensive way of communication, usually reserved for something important. The more common way was writing letters. Letter delivery took about a week. You were customarily supposed to answer a letter within a day or two, so the communication was fairly regular. When I'd be delayed with my answer, being so busy with my burlesque student life, in a couple of weeks I'd receive a telegram summoning me for a "why don't you answer the letters" phone call. My poor Mama.

Besides the dorm roommates, I befriended a few local guys who lived in the city with their families and studied in our group. One of them, Valery, became a very close friend of mine. All these friendships were initiated, of course, on the collective farm. Valery was from a working-class family; both his father and mother were working at the armory plant. He was one year older than me. Obviously, he did not make it to college on his first try but made it on the second just to avoid the military. The year between high school and college he worked at the same armory plant with his parents, so by the time we met he probably had more life experience than I did. He had a circle of his own friends and introduced me to this group. I quickly became accepted. I was from a different place, foreign to them, and therefore interesting. These city guys were spiritually closer to me than the country guys from the dorm. They were under the huge influence of nearby Moscow and some rudimentary level of dissent was certainly brewing in their minds. Hanging out with that group, I met Tatyana.

Tatyana

No sooner met but they looked,
No sooner looked but they loved . . .
William Shakespeare

The first time we met was at a gathering where she came with one of the guys from my college group. I did not like this guy and, as I found out later, neither did she. My first impression was close to shock. She looked beautiful and very bright. Her eyes were huge, rather gray than blue, and with a constant fire burning inside. When she looked at me, I could almost feel the flaring ambers touching my skin. Our kids later inherited those eyes. The girls in Tula generally did not look that pretty (I have to admit though, that at seventeen all of them nevertheless were very attractive) and she definitely stood out. As was customary in those days, and unfortunately for me, since she came to the gathering with that guy, she left the gathering with that same guy. I did not know it, but that evening happened to be their last date.

The next time we met was on a city bus a few weeks later. I was with my buddy Valery, she was going to some concert with her girlfriend Natasha. We approached to say hello and got a furious reply, something to the effect that we were both asses and could go away. If during the first meeting the flares from her eyes were just touching my skin, this time they were burning my skin all the way through. I was sure that all this wrath was pointed at my buddy rather than me because I thought that maybe Valery ran into her at some point in their common circles between now and the last time I saw her and said something stupid, or something like that. I kept thinking about this episode for another couple days and then decided to ask Valery what he did and what happened. The reply was that he had no idea, that she had lately started behaving weird and if I wanted to find out, I could call her and ask myself. This conversation took place in his parents' apartment, so when I asked for a number, he picked up the phone and called that guy Vlad from our group with whom she showed up at the first gathering. To my surprise, when he heard that I was asking for Tatyana's number, Vlad gave us the number with a wish for good luck.

Later, when we were already dating, Tatyana explained that on the bus she was actually mad at me and not at Valery, who turned out to be just an innocent bystander suffering on behalf of his buddy. Why? Because I did not call her right away. This is the ironclad logic I have happily live with ever since.

As soon as I got the number, I left Valery and ran to the nearest phone booth. My second surprise of the day was that she recognized me right away and agreed to meet that weekend at the city dancing club. As I found out later, my Kiev accent betrayed me at the first phrase.

What I called "the city dancing club" was a hangout place for local city youth. The Tula Trade Union Palace biweekly, if I remember correctly, was granting its main assembly hall to the public. The chairs were removed, and the hall was turned into a huge dancing floor. Sometimes there was a local band playing, sometimes just discs. All songs were of course pre-approved by the censorship—sorry, no Beatles or Rolling Stones. I do not recall if we were paying any entry fees, but if we did it was minimal. The crowd was always pretty much the same, after a few times you'd start recognizing the familiar faces. I never saw the guys from my dorm at these gatherings, but since I was there a couple times before with Valery, I figured that my face was already familiar enough and that I should not have any problems going there alone.

She came with another girlfriend, Luba. I was a little puzzled with the presence of Luba, but the bottom line was that she came.

A note. As it turned out, she could not come alone because it could have been taken as a wrong message. Blessed is the Lord who created the girls and the boys so different, otherwise life would be so boring.

As everyone can imagine, not much dancing happened that night. I am a horrible dancer even with one girl, two were definitely out of my league. We stood in the corner and tried to talk for maybe half an hour, but it was too loud, and we decided to leave. After we successfully seated Luba into the tramway at the nearest station and sent her home, poor Luba, we were finally left alone. We walked across the city to the place she lived, talking on the way about everything in the world—about the families, about the books, about the past, about the future—amazed how easy the communication was for both of us. Then we stood for another couple hours at the entrance to her high-rise apartment building to continue talking.

I found out that she was one year older than me, a whopping eighteen. She studied in the local College of Cultural Education. Her family was from Yaroslavl, a more northeastern region of Russia on the Volga river. This explained the different look. Her father was transferred by work when she was eight, but she never liked Tula. All the extended family—grandma, aunts, and cousins—remained in Yaroslavl. Needless to say, I told her how I missed my Kiev, and she understood. And so on. The mutual comprehension was unbelievable. We could talk for hours, walking in the park or on the street, or sitting somewhere quietly on the bench.

We started seeing each other not just regularly, but as often as possible. We showed up to all the gatherings together, I got to know better all her friends, including of course Luba and Natasha, she got to know my friends, including those from the dorm. But most often we tried to stay alone because we did not really need anyone.

There is not much to say about the next couple years in the context of this story. In the fall of 1974 our military department classes started and I had to cut my hair short. I spent too much time with Tatyana and got a couple of low grades in the summer session of 1975 but was able to bring them up at the retake. My friend Valery dropped out and was drafted. Life was a little hungry, but fun. I did not feel any anti-Semitism in Tula. Of course, I met people who did not like Jews, but they also did not like Ukrainians, Caucasians, Germans, Tatars, and so on. Russia was more multinational than Ukraine, and I was happily lost in the mix of "others." To my surprise Tatyana had quite a few Jewish friends, her best friend Natasha for example, turned out to be Jewish. Since I was the only Jew in my Mining Department and in the dorm, I was surprised to meet any in Tula, but there they were.

Once, I believe it was in 1975, when we came back after the summer break, the instructors in the military department informed us that the State of Israel was added to the list of our potential military adversaries. Before it was always the U.S., Great Britain, and West Germany. All exercises were on German territory using the leftover maps from WWII. But now Israel, wow! I was so proud. The Melikha must have gotten their asses kicked somewhere really badly if they decided to add the tiny Israel to this impressive list! I looked around in a hope of meeting another pair of proud eyes but realized that I was alone . . . (somewhere around that time I was reading the Baba Shura's Old Testament with the cross).

Every summer break, starting after the second year, we had an industrial practice for a month. Kind of like an internship, but with pay and in a hands-on working position. Our mining department was usually sending us to work at regional coal or ore quarries as helpers to the excavator machinists. I liked these practices, this was the opportunity to earn some extra money, but it was cutting the summer breaks short.

I missed Kiev, my Kiev, the place where I was born and grew up. We lived on the outskirts of the Pechersk district. The district was considered very elite, most of the government buildings were situated there and it was natural that most of the government officials and the party elite lived there as well. Our neighborhood was in the more middle-class, more remote part of the district called Pechersky Most, with several industrial plants nearby, but close enough to the center, about twenty minutes on the trolley bus.

A note. Sharing the district with the elite allowed the dwellers an access to the crumbs from the elite's tables. Even the common stores in our area were receiving a better supply than those outside the Pechersk. But there was one special store, locals named it "The Leftovers." The truth was that the party and the government elites were receiving most of their food supply from the special distribution centers closed to the public, not from the common stores. The unused surplus food from those distribution centers was sometimes sold the next day in that store. The locals knew about it, hence the name. The store was a couple of bus stops from where we lived and sometimes Mom would go there in the morning to stand in line and wait in hope that something would show up; it was like going fishing.

We lived in a five-story brick building with three stairwell sections. Each section contained twenty flats, with sixty flats total in the building. I am intentionally using the British word "flat" instead of the more common American English "apartment" because it better describes the units we lived at. Apartment is too big of a word for it. Our flat was on the fifth floor, sorry, no elevators. The flat was 25.5 square meters (275 sq. ft). Two rooms, a kitchen and a bathroom. The building was built in the early '60s for the workers of one of the local industrial plants. By agreement, the construction crew got two flats in the building; this is how my father got it. Our city block was fairly big and included a school and a public bathhouse, with the school stadium in the middle. Our building was next to the bathhouse and its boiler structure, this is where we usually played soccer as kids.

When I was coming home for the college breaks, I would walk the streets, look at the trees which were rare in Tula, watch the birds, and breathe in the primeval air. The sky was bluer, the air was sweeter, the weather was warmer. I would see the familiar faces around me—the neighbors, the store clerks, the kids from our block who had grown up in the past couple years. I felt that even street dogs knew me and were not barking at me. I definitely wanted to come back. The only missing element was Tatyana. I was missing Tatyana in Kiev and I was missing Kiev with Tatyana. The logical solution was to come back with her.

In the middle of my third year of college, I decided that it was time for us to make it official. We both agreed that we would get married a few months into our dating, but the fact that we were both students presented a major obstacle. At that time my study in the college stabilized, I was sure that I would graduate without problems in a couple years. Tatyana was almost done with her studies and was graduating the next summer.

The trigger to our decision was an event that happened to Tatyana's close family friends. Their family also moved to Tula from Yaroslavl during the same transfer, both fathers were working at the same printing plant of regional newspaper. The families kept very close ties.

A note. The newspapers in Soviet Union were the arm of the Communist Party, including the printing plants. Propaganda was taken very seriously by the Melikha, all the editors and so-called journalists were party members by default. The workers at the printing plants were thoroughly checked for fear of deliberate misprinting and were getting a higher pay and better benefits than the other workers.

I am telling this story the way I heard it and saw it. Some people may say that it could not have happened and that they all pretended. Maybe, I don't know. Even then there were some skeptics.

The family had a sixteen-year-old daughter who attended a trade school. One day she came to the local clinic and complained about the pain in her stomach. She was immediately taken to the hospital and in a few hours delivered a healthy baby girl. My Tatyana was the one who received the phone call from the delivery room. The girl was afraid to give her mother's phone number. Apparently, the family did not know anything about her pregnancy. Later, after the fact, her mother admitted that there were some alarming signs in the girl's behavior—for example she did not allow her to enter the bathroom when she was taking a shower, but all was written off to a teenage weirdness. Anyways, the family quickly found the seventeen-year-old "author," contacted his parents, and arranged the marriage, which the law allowed under those circumstances. Tatyana, as a major participant in this happily ending story, was invited to the wedding and I came with her. There, sitting at this unusual wedding, I suddenly realized that we were together for two years already, that I did not want to look like this fool, and that it was not fair for her to wait any longer.

The formal proposal, the way we know it now, was not customary back then. It was like:

"Hey, let's get married."

"OK, let's do."

Now we just had to convince our parents.

My Biblical Ruth

First, I had to talk to my parents. I believe it was a long weekend of New Year's Day of 1976 when I took a flight home. There was a direct flight between Tula and Kiev, not that expensive with the student discount. My parents were a little surprised when I showed up because the winter break was supposed to start in mid-January and I had another couple weeks of study. When they heard that I wanted to get married they promptly fell into shock. They knew of course that I was dating a girl in Tula, but I had not turned twenty yet and had not finished college. The early marriages during the last year of college or right after were pretty common back then, but this was a bit too early.

"Is she pregnant?"

"No."

"Then what is the rush?"

"What is the difference now or a year later?"

"How are you gonna feed the family? You will have to drop out and go to work!"

"To the contrary, we will live on the same money, I will continue my studies, we will just be together."

"You are together now, wait a couple years, she can wait!"

"Wait for what?"

And so on, and so forth. Another problem was that she was Russian. Better than Ukrainian, but still not Jewish. This was Mom's biggest concern. That "she will cheat on you," that "I wanted a daughter in the family and you are bringing a stranger," and "I don't know how we will get along." I told her what probably every man tells his mother: "Mom, you have to see her, she is so beautiful, as soon as you see her, you will love her, too!" Poor Mama . . . But I have to admit that later on they got along well.

My father's concern was mostly about dropping out of college. His dream for me to get higher education was so close, and now he saw my marriage as putting that in jeopardy. I still do not understand why. Dropping out of college meant immediate draft into the military for two years, and I do not know how any newlywed wife would allow this to happen, certainly not Tatyana.

After a couple days of arguments, Dad brought in the heavy artillery, his cousin and my uncle Semion. Uncle Semion was a former navy sailor, funny and at the same time a pretty tough guy. My parents knew that I respected him and, therefore, may listen. After going through the second round of the same arguments, Uncle Semion told my father that there was nothing he could do, and to not forget to invite him to the wedding.

When I flew back from Kiev, Tatyana and I started working on the second challenge ahead of us—her parents. They had met me, of course, many times in the two years we were dating, but I was not sure how seriously they were taking me. Plus, there was a flip side of the same coin that she was Russian, and I was Jewish. My worry was that for them to give their only daughter to a Jew was to doom her life to additional unnecessary straggles. As it turned out, they were not even thinking this way. So, Tatyana picked the evening when both of them were home, I bought a cake and a bouquet of flowers, and showed up to ask for her hand in marriage. The situation was awkward, as it usually is in those circumstances. The father was stunned, I could see he did not expect it. As I later learned, he always had a delayed reaction, so that evening he could not manifest anything intelligible. The mother, to the contrary, was very engaged. I could feel that she took it in a positive way, but she remained calm and gave us a very logical response, that they were happy and had no objections, but since I was still a student, they wanted to talk to my parents. This was as good response as we could have hoped for, and we moved on with our plan.

With consent from my parents I invited Tatyana to come with me to Kiev for the winter break. The break was for about ten days. I introduced her to my parents, to my older sister, and to my friends who happened to be there at that time. The family took to her and were very friendly, I was so happy. Tatyana put on all efforts and really looked gorgeous. I could see behind the worry some curiosity sparkled in Mom's eyes.

Tatyana fell in love with Kiev from day one. I showed her everything I could in those few days. Now we were walking together, breathing that primeval air together, and looking together at that gray winter sky. The city now had two amorous idiots instead of one.

We returned to Tula with my father, he met her parents and the deal was done. We went to the city hall and filled out the application, the waiting line was for a couple months, so the date was set for March 6.

The applications were taken on certain days—I believe it was Wednesday, during the working hours. That day I had the Explosive Technics and Materials class. Our instructor did not allow anyone to cut any of his lectures, as this was his major pre-requirement for passing the course. His reasoning was very simple: "You calculate the explosives the way I taught you, then you prepare the blast the way I taught you, then you lighten up the cord, and then . . . Baams! You do not know what to do next because you missed

57

my class!" Made perfect sense. So, we planned everything in advance. Tatyana took the line in the city hall and was waiting for me. I took a seat in the classroom next to the exit and as soon as the lecture was over, ran, took a taxi and barely made it before the office was closed.

The wedding was at her parents' apartment. From my side there were my parents, Uncle Misha, Uncle Semion, and couple of my friends from college. On Tatyana's side I met her aunts and cousins from Yaroslavl and cousins from Leningrad. Natasha and Luba of course were there. Her extended family were very friendly; only one cousin Lussia, from Leningrad, whispered in her ear, "What are you doing marrying a Jew?" Well, that confirmed the rumors about Leningrad. On the other hand, her other cousin and Lussia's older brother Vitaly, who was a pretty high-ranking official in Leningrad, told her not to listen to anyone, follow her heart, and that everything would be good. This cousin Vitaly was much older than us, probably in his late forties. Later he helped us a lot when we were emigrating.

Now it's time to tell about the most important aspect of that episode, the point that went very casual, but probably played the key role in all future events. When we were filling out our applications in the city hall, one of the questions was which last name the groom and the bride were taking. The law allowed both male and female to take the spouse's last name. Not the nationality, but the last name. Many mixed marriages with one Jewish counterpart were taking Russian, Ukrainian, Armenian, or any other last names available just to make life easier. So, this was my opportunity to blend in, but in my mind, this was not even an option. Remember, I'd already read Baba Shura's Old Testament with the cross, how could I betray all those generations who lived before me? So, my part was easy. But to my surprise Tatyana told me that she wanted to take my very Jewish last name. This was shocking and unheard of! This would doom her to all the suffering and deprivations of my people without any practical benefit.

"Are you sure?" I asked her.

"Yes, I am sure. Your people are my people. I do not want our children to grow up being ashamed of their father, I am taking your last name. Done!"

I was very humbled. Is that not what the Biblical Ruth said to her mother-in-law? Your people are my people . . . Not only was I getting a wife, a friend, and a companion, I was getting a soulmate, a partner in crime.

A note. She never went through a formal conversion. To me, the statement she made in that city hall was her formal conversion. She lived with me and the rest of us in anti-Semitic Kiev for twelve years, gave birth to two kids with Jewish last names, got them through kindergartens and schools, lived there with her Jewish last name, worked there with her Jewish last name, went with us through emigration and immigration . . . She was with us as a Jew on the front lines, in the lines of fire! What other conversion does a person need? How can you explain all that happened to us to the American court of rabbis? Maybe this story will . . . All these years we were afraid that the formal conversion would be too formal, would downgrade what we had, would turn her from a romantic Biblical Ruth to just another ordinary convert. She lights the Shabbat candles as a Jewish woman, sits in the synagogue with other Jewish women and prays with other Jewish women to our Creator G-d. Both of her children considered themselves Jewish and went through formal conversion. Maybe our reasoning for not doing the formal conversion makes us not religious enough . . . Maybe later? Well, He who knows everything will sort it out.

After the wedding I moved in with her parents but continued paying for the dorm to keep my temporary dorm registration, which preserved my permanent Kiev registration, leaving us a chance to come back to Kiev.

Their apartment was slightly larger than ours, an impressive 33 square meters. The same two rooms, a kitchen and a bathroom. Now that all the time that I previously spent on dating Tatyana and searching for food was freed up, I could dedicate it to my studying and my grades sharply improved. That summer session was the first time I passed all my tests with the straight "5." The easiest subject for me was "Electrical Power Distribution Network for Mining Installations." Most of the mining machinery, at least back then, was operating at 3KV, therefore power distribution was very important. For me the subject was very logical, hence easy. Plus, I was pulling those 3KV cables with my own hands when we moved the excavators during my summer practices. Little did I know that this would become my primary engineering specialty in the future.

In the fall of 1977 Tatyana gave birth to our beautiful daughter; we named her Masha. I was 21, could not believe my eyes looking at this miracle smiling at me. This is the point in a man's life when the world turns upside down and the little "me" inside of him suddenly becomes a big "US." Tatyana was 22, it was customary for a woman to have her first baby at that age, so she and her family were very happy and became very busy.

I graduated college in the summer of 1978 and within a couple days was summoned for the military camps. Masha made her first steps toward me the day I had to leave, it sucked, but a man's got to do . . .

At the camps we were dressed in the military uniform and were called cadets. For three months we lived in the tents, used a trench as an outhouse, marched, served in the kitchen, and dug our fortification exercises manually with the shovel. About a week into the term we had our military oath of allegiance.

A note. The oath began with the words "I, Zinovy Gutman, a citizen of the Union of Soviet Socialist Republics, facing my comrades, am solemnly giving this oath," and so on. When the Jews, and only the Jews, were emigrating in the late '70s and the late '80s, the Melikha stripped us of our Soviet citizenship. Therefore, the oath was annulled not by me, but by the other party. In addition, in the early '90s the U.S.S.R. ceased to exist. So, when I was naturalized as a United States citizen and took my oath of allegiance, I was absolutely free from any other previously taken oaths.

I still remember the 15-kilometers marching drill in full ammunition somewhere in the middle of the term. I mean with an AK machine gun, with munition, with the shovel, and with the rolled trench-coat across the shoulder. That damned shovel and the trench coat. The given task was to cross the finish line in full complement, meaning that if one member of the group did not make it, none in the group passes. We were just students, some of us in better shape than the others, some just completely out of shape. That was fun, the last kilometer we were just dragging each other in the dust, but we all made it. After that exercise our two-kilometers morning runs, with which I was struggling every day, became a joy.

In the camps was the first time I bumped into the completely unexpected real anti-Semitic episode in Russia, and it did not come from the military. A couple weeks into the term, right after the oath, some people began disappearing. Everyone who had connections was being transferred back to the city to continue training at the department, probably 10 to 20% of us were gone. So, the Tatars, and there were quite a few of them, started going around the camp and yapping that all the "Jews" left and now all of us must serve for them. Dudes, what are you talking about? I am the only Jew in the department and I am still here!

Well, everything comes to an end, and so did the camp. I passed my test with the "excellent" grade, received the rank of lieutenant in reserve, and returned back home to my girls. Now was the hardest part of somehow getting to Kiev.

The rule was that every graduating student had to work for two years at the place of assignment before he or she could work at their place of choice, with the exception of special circumstances. I should not repeat myself by saying that the "special circumstances" were reserved for those with special connections. The assignments were distributed in the institute during those couple days between graduation and the military camps in order of grade-average ranks. So, if any industrial plant or a mine or a quarry wanted to employ a young specialist, they would send a request. A student with the best grade average would enter the room first and pick his or her choice where to go. Naturally, the places that wanted to receive the best students would add some perks, like a promise of an apartment. I had a pretty good average and was entering the room third in the Mining Department.

We developed a conspiracy plan to beat the system. I asked Uncle Misha if he could send a request from the Mining Rescue Detachment. This was not a very attractive request and, when I entered the assignment room after the first two guys, I easily found it on the table. The Assignment Commission was a little surprised that I chose that but had no objections. So, as soon as I returned from my military camps, I went to the place of my assignment. It was a typical small mining town in the Tula region. I found Uncle Misha and he took me straight to the detachment's medical office for a checkup. The doctor performed a routine medical checkup on me and told Uncle Misha that with all due respect, his nephew (I was presented as a nephew) could not work in the detachment because of weak vision. We played a little disappointment, I took written rejection papers, thanked Uncle Misha and went back to Tula. As expected, all assignments in the institute were already distributed, which created "special circumstances" for me, and I received my free diploma with the right to work at the place of my choice, exactly as was planned.

As I had mentioned earlier, with all our love for Kiev, Tatyana and I would not have minded taking an assignment and working at a quarry somewhere for a couple years to earn some money. But we wanted at least a chance to be able to return to Kiev. With the system of mandatory residence registration, we would not have that chance.

That was the end of our Russian period. Looking back, I can sincerely say thank you to Russia, and I mean the Russian people, not Soviet Melikha, for five years of my youth, for friends, for education, for language, for diverse experiences, and of course for my beautiful wife and daughter. And sorry for taking away the best of your genetic pool.

A note. Did we cheat to get to Kiev? Well, the Melikha created all those ridiculous rules not with intent that the people would follow them, but with intent that the people would be forced to break them, enabling the Melikha to have better control over the population by forgiving or punishing at will. (This thought I borrowed from Ayn Rand's Atlas Shrugged, in which she described this subject in detail.)

The Mishpukha

(The Family)

Now it's probably the perfect time to tell a little more about my family, the family that Tatyana was about to face. The stories I am about to tell came from some family legends, which I will try to put into historical perspective to the best of my knowledge, but I cannot guarantee their accuracy.

My father's side came from Korosten, a small town northwest of Kiev not far from the border with Belarus. For a better understanding of the historical situation in that region at the turn of the twentieth century, I must explain that under the tsar's rule the Jewish population in those little towns and villages in Ukraine and Belarus lived in extreme poverty. I cannot say that Ukrainian population lived much better, otherwise there would have been be no revolutions, but at least they were allowed to work on the land, were not restricted in movement, and were not the subject of periodic pogroms. As far as I know, my great grandfather Yakov had a man-driven mill and made his living out of that mill. It is quite possible that he served in the tsar's army and bought this mill using the money received at discharge. During the revolution, the Bolsheviks decided that the mill was private property and expropriated it. Yakov was declared a "kulak," which in revolutionary jargon meant a bourgeois, and was deprived not only of his property, but also of all his civil rights. He was lucky that they did not send him to the labor camps. I cannot blame Ukrainians for that crime; those were fellow revolutionary Jews. Later on, my grandfather bought Yakov a little house near the river and he lived there with his second wife. My dad remembers visiting them as a kid. Yakov perished during WWII. As a former kulak he was not eligible for evacuation ahead of the advancing Nazi armies and stayed in Korosten. When the surviving family members came back after the war, there were some strangers living in the house who claimed that they did not know anything. Some neighbors told them that the local Ukrainian Nazi collaborators executed the old couple right there in their backyard. Were the people who killed them the same people who lived in their house? Who knows . . .

My grandfather Zelik was Yakov's youngest of three kids with his first wife, my great grandmother. Unfortunately, I do not know her name. She died young and Yakov married his second wife. He had several children from the second marriage, one of them was my great aunt, Fannie, who lived in Kiev (Tatyana had a chance to meet her). Zelik's older sister Rivka emigrated to America right after the revolution. The story I've heard about Rivka goes like this:

There was a man in their village who went to America to earn some money, leaving his wife and kids behind with the intention of bringing them later, after he at least somewhat established himself, a pretty common story in those days. Some of those stories had happy endings, read for example Golda Meir's mémoires; others ended up in tragedy. While the family was waiting, the wife died, leaving kids in that village practically orphans. So, the man wrote to the community with the outcry asking that someone please bring his children to him, that he would pay expenses and do all he could in appreciation. Rivka was a maiden and decided that she would help this man. Remember, it was very little fun living in Ukraine during those times: the revolution, the civil war, hunger, and pogroms on the top. She took the kids and delivered them to this man in America. The man married her, and they lived happily ever after, having more kids between them. This is how things were done back then.

Zelik was planning to follow his sister but met my grandmother Golda and got stuck in Korosten. Golda was the oldest sister of a bunch of the semi-orphaned siblings and could not go. I know that there was a great grandmother Gitl, but never heard about the great grandfather, he had probably perished in one of the wars or pogroms.

Zelik's middle brother moved to the Far East of Russia in the late 1920s, where on the border with China, Stalin was establishing a Jewish autonomous region. His far-stretching plans were to eventually move all the Jewish population there. We had a whole bunch of relatives there in the Far East, all of whom now live in Israel.

A note. Fortunately for all of us, Stalin's plans to transfer Jews were not destined to be. The dictator croaked right at the early stages of the execution of his plan. Would he succeed, half of the Jewish population of the Soviet Union would perish in the 1950s, a few years after the Nazi Holocaust. This is a very little-known modern Purim story, worthy of another book by future historians.

Zelik was completely illiterate but was a born businessman. He started as a carrier with one horse, delivering cargo from the local railroad station to the construction sites. Then, as my father remembered, he had several horses, then the horses disappeared and instead of delivering, Zelik started supplying materials, buying the high-grade lumber in western Ukraine for coal mines in the eastern Donbas region. My understanding is that all this happened in the late '20s during the New Economic Policy, when the Communists allowed small-business enterprises, kind of like modern China's economic model. This New Economic Policy lasted a few years and ended with brutal Stalin's repressions of the '30s. With this money made on trading lumber, Zelik built a house for himself, bought a little house for his father and stepmother, and helped his siblings, and his wife's siblings. When I was a child, we visited Korosten a few times and stayed in Zelik's old house, where one of my great aunties was living. I remember it was near the railroad station and next to the farmers market. The house had a big orchard where Golda, for a short while, had chicken and geese, and everything they could have ever dreamed of.

All fun abruptly ended when in the early '30s NKVD (the predecessor of KGB) came and arrested Zelik. He had not committed any crime. His problem was that his sister lived in America. At that time the Melikha was busy expropriating from the population all the gold and hard currency they could get their hands on for the noble purpose of industrialization. The boys in the local NKVD probably received an ambitious order from the top of how many dollars they must collect and remembered about Zelik. Again, all those were fellow Jews from the same village, they knew everything about each other. When Zelik said no, he would not write a letter to his sister with the request for dollars, they threw him into the local dungeon. When the family found out what happened, Yakov wrote a letter to Rivka and asked for the ransom money to free her brother. Apparently, the NKVD boys knew what they were doing! When the money arrived, the family faced another challenge of how to pass the information to Zelik that the money was here, and he should agree. Well, the youngest and the bravest sister, Auntie Fannie, whom we met in Kiev, arranged a scandal in some public place big enough to get arrested for a cooldown and was able to pass a note to Zelik.

But wait! That was not the end of the story. In a few months after Zelik's release, the guys naturally came back for more money. This time Zelik did not wait to be arrested and ran away. While Golda and the kids were bullshitting the unwanted guests at the door, Zelik managed to climb to the attic and then escaped through the roof to the orchard and out. Why through the attic and the roof I do not know, this is what my father told me. Now, being a fugitive, he hid for a few months at his cousin's in a neighboring town, until it became known and then escaped to Kiev. Somehow, he found a job and settled in Kiev and after a while, when it became safe, moved his family there. You may ask how was it possible, was not NKVD looking for him? My guess is that historically at that time there were brutal cleansings within the Bolshevik's party. The "Stalinistas" were killing the "Trotskystas," and so on. Those guys who came to arrest Zelik were probably themselves executed a few months later somewhere in the NKVD dungeons, and those who executed them were later killed, too.

Fortunately, they were too busy killing each other to look for a guy who just did not want to pay a ransom.

Both Zelik and Golda died during the war; he was 41 and she was 39. I never got to meet them. The war started in June 1941, the German troops were advancing very rapidly and by August were already approaching Kiev. All industrial plants, all equipment and machinery that could be salvaged, was loaded on the railroad carts and sent east. Here I have to give it to the Soviet leadership that they allowed the Jewish population to be evacuated. I am not sure how exactly it worked, I believe they just pulled a bunch of cargo trains to the railroad stations and let anyone who wanted to load up and head east and then later sorted them out. Very few Ukrainians left, it was mostly Jewish refugees. All young men at the age of sixteen and up were drafted. Those who could not serve yet were just moved east to prevent them from being drafted by Germans.

So, Golda with her older daughter, my Aunt Ada, loaded the train and headed east, ending up in Siberia. My father was sixteen and was drafted. He told me that from the military commissary they just walked east accompanied by officers, across the Dnieper river and on for another twenty kilometers before they were loaded into the railroad cargo carts at the Darnitsa station. At the entrance to the bridge all the parents were turned away, but Zelik talked to the officers and somehow managed to walk with the group up to Darnitsa. This was the last time my dad saw his father. Once I asked him what they were talking about.

"You walked together for hours, what did he tell you?"

"You know what," my father answered, "I do not remember. I was too embarrassed in front of the other guys that my father was walking with us . . . Something about my mother spoiling me too much and, now, how am I going to survive."

A note. Is not this conversation amazing? It can be easily placed into any time in the history anywhere in the world. An eternal worry of a man about his son. And eternal ignorance of youth.

But my father did survive. As I am writing these words, my dad is still alive at ninety-three and lives with us in the U.S.

After everyone left, Zelik was drafted too and took part in the military debacle on the eastern bank of the Dnieper river near Kiev, where Germans surrounded and methodically annihilated several Soviet divisions. After the war, some former neighbors told my dad and Ada that they saw Zelik in Kiev, carrying some other wounded man in the crowd marching to the Baby Yar, where all of them were killed by the Nazis. This is as much as we know. I can guess that surviving the debacle, he and his wounded comrade would probably try to go east, but most likely found all roads blocked by the German troops and had to turn west and return to Kiev, where they found their death. My parents named me Zinovy in his memory (the name Zelik was too Jewish to survive) and, apparently, it became my destiny to fulfill his dreams and move to America.

Grandma Golda died the same winter in Siberia when she went to the forest to pick some wood and got into a snowstorm. She was with another younger evacuee woman who happened to be pregnant. Another woman made it back to the village practically unconscious, most likely the urge to save the baby gave her extra strength. But grandma fell asleep. Later in the spring, when the snow melted, seventeen-years-old Ada, with the help of the locals, was trying to find her body to bury, but all the efforts were in vain.

My father Efim's story is worthy of a separate book, but in short, their train from Darnitsa got under the German aviation bombardment and was destroyed. The boys from his neighborhood formed a gang of eight friends and started moving eastward, away from the approaching front line. There was an interesting episode when the front line outran them, and they were caught in some Ukrainian village in the no-man's-land. The Soviet army had already left, but the Nazi army had not come yet. The local villagers armed themselves and were waiting to serve the approaching Nazis. So, they detained the boys and immediately started wondering if there were any Jews among them. There were two, my dad and another guy, but the friends did not give them away. The Nazi collaborators picked one, who was actually a Ukrainian but had a darker complexion, and locked him in the barn telling the others to go away. Can you imagine? This Ukrainian guy in this grave situation did not say anything, did not betray his Jewish friends. Can we jumble all Ukrainians into one pile with Nazi collaborators after that? The closure was simple. The gang waited until the guard fell asleep after drinking their moonshine, picked the lock, got their friend and ran away.

The guys ended up working in some mine in Donbas. When the front line approached again, they moved further east where at some point the group split. My dad accidentally found his grandmother and a bunch of other female relatives from Korosten who just happened to be evacuated to this region of Russia and started working on the collective farm with them. There they showed him a letter from his sister Ada, in which he found out what happened to their mother. Suddenly he decided that he had to go and find his sister in Siberia. That was a very long and very difficult journey; he almost died from starvation. At the end he found Ada and settled in some Siberian Cossack village, where with the other local seventeen-years-old guys was assigned to the Cossack Cavalry unit for the preparatory military training. Just imagine a paradox of the city Jewish boy serving in the Cossack Cavalry unit. On the other hand, I had a couple of Cossack buddies in my dorm at college. Nothing special, ordinary Russian guys, especially when sober. Vodka made them a little more violent, but overall, they were OK.

A historical note. Cossacks were free settlers in the bordering southern regions of the Russian Empire dated to approximately the 15th to the 16th centuries. Contrary to the feudal serfdom peasants in the mainland Russia, they enjoyed limited self-governing in return for military service to the Russian crown. As a result, Cossack Cavalry units had an ill fame of crushing the working-class protests and strikes during the revolution and taking a leading part in the bloody Jewish pogroms (raids on Jewish villages and neighborhoods accompanied with killings, rapes, lynching, looting, and complete destruction). Ever since in Jewish historic memory and folklore Cossacks were always topping the list of villains until they were replaced by Nazis after World War II.

There, in the Siberian Cossacks village, my father, then seventeen-year-old Efim, found in the local newspaper an advertisement from the Railroad Construction Technical School and sent in an application along with another guy from that village. They were both accepted and moved to that school in Kazakhstan. The school deferred the military draft, and then the war was over.

An interesting episode happened to Efim on his journey to Siberia. He had to cross the Volga River near Stalingrad. The year was 1942 and the front line was rapidly approaching the city, where one of the largest WWII battles was about to unfold. The Volga in that region is several miles wide, and to get to the east bank of the river he had to take a ferry, which was really just a flat-deck barge. Sitting on that crowded barge he pulled a piece of a dried bread crust his grandma gave him for the journey and suddenly saw an old man looking at him with hungry eyes. So Efim shared his crust with the old man. Soon after that the German airplanes came out of nowhere and started bombarding the ferry and everything else they could find on the surface of the river. The immediate instinct was to run away, so some people started jumping overboard. My dad could swim and was about to jump, too, but the old man stopped him. "Son," he said, "do not jump. Those in the water, consider them already dead, but on the barge, we still have a chance to survive. We will be killed only from a direct hit and so far, they are missing."

The man was probably right because besides the shrapnel and miles to swim, the sound waves from the exploding bombs would definitely shock the swimmer unconscious and he would certainly drown. This story shows how far a piece of a shared bread crust can take you, sometimes saving your life.

***

On my mother's side the family came from Kanev, a little town south of Kiev down the Dnieper river. My grandfather Solomon was from a blacksmith family. He, his father, and all his brothers were blacksmiths, with the corresponding last name of Shtockmeister. Solomon was tall, probably six feet or more, with fair hair, blue eyes—the typical Ashkenazi look. Sometimes I wonder where I missed a golden deposit of genes with my five-foot-five? Grandma Hiya was a small, very quiet, very kind lady with unconditional love for all of us, her grandchildren. Solomon died from a stroke in 1975, and Tatyana did not have a chance to meet him; grandma passed away in 1979, so Tatyana and Masha met her. Solomon and Hiya had two daughters, my mother Sonya and my aunt, Raya. Raya had three children, my cousins, all of whom now live in Israel.

Solomon and Hiya's story was much simpler. Before the war Solomon was working in the defense industrial plant in Kiev. The plant with all its workers and their families was evacuated to Siberia, where they were manufacturing tanks for the war.

Grandpa Solomon was a staunch Communist. Being from a poor family, he sincerely believed that the Soviet Power did everything to help the working people. His argument was that under the tsar's rule we were hungry and illiterate and now we have food on the table and our children go to school. As a child I remember how Raya's husband, uncle Zunia, was always arguing with Solomon about all that. Zunia was a war veteran, working as an engineer in some research center. His opinions sharply differed from the official mainstream, but were very logical and made sense to me. This was probably my first exposure to dissent.

A note. I never had a chance to argue with my grandpa, but if I could I would say that for our food and schools for children we had to pay the ultimate price: our freedom.

An interesting story happened to Solomon's brother, Uncle Ziama or Uncle Vanya—he actually had two names. Once my mom explained to me why. During the war Ziama was planted at the Nazi-occupied territory with the underground resistance group. For conspiracy purposes he posed as a Russian Orthodox priest in the re-opened church under the name of Vanya. You may ask, why him? Because as a kid he attended a few years of an elementary Jewish religious school, a heder, and therefore better than others fit the profile. Apparently, it did not last long before he blew the cover as an imposter and went into hiding in the house of a young Ukrainian woman named Irene somewhere in a rural Ukrainian village. It is not clear if she was part of the resistance group or just a sympathizer. Pretty soon they became lovers, and she hid her Vanya for two to three years of the occupation. After the war they came back to Kiev, got married and lived together the rest of their lives. I remember visiting them as a kid, my cousins in Israel even have a photo of all of us. For Irene he always remained "Vanya."

The Crucible

Socialism is Soviet Power plus the electrification of the whole country. (Lenin)

The electrification of the whole country is Socialism minus Soviet Power. (People's wisdom based on a simple math)

In the fall of 1978 I returned to Kiev. The plan was that Tatyana and Masha would stay with her parents in Tula until I found a job, otherwise there could be problems with her permanent-residence registration.

A note. Unemployment as such did not exist in the Soviet Union. There was always a need for working hands everywhere in any industrial plant and on any construction site. I am not talking about the party boss's positions, I am talking about the positions where the people were really doing some work. I'd explain it by the low productivity and low salaries. Not working, except for women with children, was considered an act of parasitism, a crime punished by a prison term for couple years in the labor camps. By the way, a famous Russian poet and Nobel Prize laureate Joseph Brodsky was arrested by the Melikha for parasitism and sentenced to the labor camps because writing poems that were not approved by the censorship was not considered a job.

I took my first shot at the Kiev Metro Construction for any position available, junior engineer or assistant construction manager, since it was directly related to what I studied in college. Trying to help, my dad found that a father of one of his construction buddies, a retired colonel, was working in the Metro Human Resources. I came directly to this man, showed my credentials, filled out an application, and was told to call him in a few days. I called him several times, and finally he told me to come see him. When I came over, the man closed the door and frankly asked me if I was planning to emigrate to Israel. I was shocked; it was probably written all over my face. I sincerely answered that no, I had just graduated college and was not going anywhere, plus my wife is Russian. The man smiled at my last argument and told me that the Metro is a strategic site and I did not have any chance to work here. So, this door was closed.

A note. Please remember that I was a born Soviet citizen with an officer military rank. For comparison, when we came to America a decade later as refugees, I was allowed to work at the nuclear plants and at the military bases before I even became a citizen.

Here I must give a bit of a historical perspective. With my luck, the fall of 1978, when I returned to Kiev, fell at the peak of the first wave of Jewish emigration from the Soviet Union. As a matter of fact, the first news I heard landing in Kiev was that my older sister Galina was planning to go. Huge lines, hundreds of people, were forming at the Department of Visas and Registrations (OVIR in Russian abbreviations, later there were songs written about this organization) in the center of the city, puzzling the bewildered population and provoking unneeded questions. In workplaces around the city everyone who filed an application was called to a public rally, a modern version of the medieval inquisition autodaffe, where the "traitor" had to stand alone in the middle of the stage and all coworkers had to publicly speak about him or her with condemnations. After that, by an open vote the person was fired. As I've mentioned, the organization's human resources were branches of the KGB, they always picked the person's closest friends and forced them to give those condemnation speeches. Of course, there were decent people who were too embarrassed to read these speeches, but everyone had a family to think of. I would add this to the list of crimes committed by the Melikha against its own people.

The processing of the application to emigrate took about half a year and all those people were left without any means to support themselves.

Plus, not everyone was getting permission to go. There were many denials based on relatives having access to "secret" information or place of military service or based on nothing at all. People were taking huge, huge risks for a simple hope.

At that time neither I nor Tatyana were even thinking about emigration. All we wanted was to find a job, earn some money, buy a little co-op unit to leave our parents alone and live our lives. We both loved Kiev, we had a bunch of friends in Kiev, we were young and ambitious and did not want to go anywhere.

So, I figured that to find a job I had to look for something less strategic than digging the tunnels for the subway trains. I visited countless organizations with references and without references with the same end result. At some point I realized that I became radioactive, but I did not give up.

A good example of what was happening to me is this episode in my search for a job. One day I was coming home from one of my unsuccessful tries and decided to walk home instead of taking the tram. Taking a shortcut, I suddenly noticed a tablet on the wall with the name of an organization I did not even know existed, The Slope Enforcement Construction. This needs some additional explanation: The City of Kiev lays on two banks of Dnieper River, which runs through it. The left bank is flat, continuing into the famous Ukrainian steppes, from which historically all the

Asian invasions had come. The right bank is very steep, this is where the ancient city was built using the steepness of the slope as a natural fortification. That the organization was enforcing that slope made absolute sense to me. Since this was what I studied in my college, I walked in. I explained to the secretary what I wanted, and she immediately took me to the manager. The manager got very excited that I had a diploma and a permanent residence and told me that they were looking for a specialist just like me, that in a half-hour he would be meeting with his construction managers and he would talk me up to them and expected to see them fighting to get me on their teams. He told me that his human resources guy was out that morning, but he would be back in the afternoon. He asked me to go back to the secretary, fill out an application, and come back in the afternoon to finish the formalities to start working tomorrow. I flew home, ate lunch and came back in the afternoon. The secretary took me to human resources and the guy asked me what I wanted. Being a little surprised, I told him that there should be my approved application somewhere on his desk and that I had already talked to the manager. The answer was that they did not have any openings. On my request to talk to the manager, he asked me to leave.

This story was typical. In one place I even started working and was rejected the next day by human resources. I am giving all these details to emphasize to the American reader that there was plenty of work for me there, and the managers would have loved to hire me, but they probably received a directive not to, or were just afraid. I was looking for a job in the U.S. during the recession, and believe me that was different.

Help came from my Uncle Semion. He knew someone at the Research Institute for Building Constructions and I was hired there as a junior engineer with salary of 110 rubles per month. The salary was the lowest imaginable, but I got a permanent job in Kiev, brought Tatyana and Masha, and that was our start.

Tatyana found a librarian job at Kiev Medical Institute pretty fast, of course by reference, for 120 rubles. Despite the questionable last name, her fifth line looked clean.

The research institute was a very interesting organization. At that time the construction industry was developing the best practices of assembling multi-story buildings from reinforced-concrete blocks. The department I was working at was responsible for developing the transportation means for delivering these blocks from the factory to the construction site. As I have mentioned, the salaries in the department were super low and they had to hire Jews because no one else would want to work there. Four out of nine workers in my department were members of the tribe. In my new place I was suddenly submerged back into that old ironically-mocking atmosphere of Kiev dissent after five years of isolation. In Tula I read the Bible, considered myself an independent thinker, and was intellectually challenging propaganda to the best of my ability. Now I realized how far had I fallen behind. There were endless puns, anecdotes, and jokes about the system with everyone, including the manager, laughing and participating. This is when the forgotten words like "Melikha" came back into my lexicon.

Half of the department were young engineers straight out of college, just like me. We formed a so-called collective farming-mourning team. It just so happened that at those times the department was constantly receiving two types of requests from the regional party committee: either send three to four people for day work at the collective farm or send the same three to four people to form a mourning crowd when some of the party bosses died. This was the duty of the youth. The collective farm work was annoying: waking up early in the morning, loading into the buses, working all day in the field, then coming back home late in the evening. The mourning duty was much easier; it usually lasted half a day after which you were free to go home. Party leaders were dropping like flies and we were always busy.

A note. Please do not blame us, dear reader, for being hard-heartened. We did not invent this idiotic and savage custom of forcing people to show their love for the rulers. Since the ancient times it had always ended up in hypocritical circus. My personal trick was to not look at the family members, just pass by the body and go home.

The life and soul of the department was our Head Project Engineer, Victor Alexandrovich Shalevich. The man was a walking encyclopedia, he knew by heart all the formulas, multipliers, and coefficients from the reference books. When he was doing calculations for the new panel-support frame, he would sit all of us young engineers around the big table and do it aloud, explaining every step. Along the way he would usually divert into vaguely related subjects, for example what if instead of the panel-supporting frame you'd have to calculate a submarine supporting frame, what would be the difference, and so on. The man was at the end of his career and yes, in the past he did calculated frames for the submarines and spacecraft. In addition, he knew several languages (to the extent of translating the printed texts): English, German, and French. And, as he would always proudly add, a little bit of Yiddish. Only the Melikha knows how this brilliant man ended up in such low-grade job with such a low salary. What a waste! Their eyes were completely fogged by their anti-Semitism, no wonder their system collapsed!

Another of Shalevich's talents was that, being short and bald, his look resembled that of Lenin. During the Communist Subbotniks (see note below) we'd always asked him to please pose. After a few rounds of cutesy refusal, he'd stand on the top of the bench stretching out his right hand, like the big guy on all the monuments, and that was the highlight of our day. Risky, but very funny.

A note. The Communist Subbotnik was an event in the Soviet Union when a Saturday, nearest to Lenin's birthday on April 22, was used as a mandatory day of free labor—I mean labor without pay. In some places people were just working in their workplaces, especially if their organization was behind schedule, but in most cases, it was cleaning the office premises or doing some landscaping. Subbotniks were presumed to be voluntary, but not participating was punished. I would not even mention this inferior abuse if I did not notice that in the modern United States someone is organizing Earth Day, very popular event in San Francisco. Earth Day always falls on Lenin's birthday on April 22 and consists—so far—of volunteer labor of cleaning parks and shorelines. People! I am in full support of volunteers devoting time to their communities, but let's move it to any other day of the year!

In relation to our emigration story, I cannot say that working in that pretty loose and open environment and communicating with those guys turned my thoughts toward emigration, but it definitely got me thinking. "Look at yourself," I thought, "look at how you live, how your family lives, look at the job you found. Do you think you will ever find a better job? Do you think it will ever get any better?" That was certainly the beginning of the awakening.

At that same time my older sister Galina was waiting for permission to leave. She and her husband Efim were in their late 20s and early 30s. They had two kids: a seven-year-old daughter and a one-year-old son. Both of them had to quit their jobs and just waited, month after month, staying in lines to check the status of their application in OVIR, living on practically nonexistent savings. Of course, my parents were helping them financially as much as they could. Unexpected help came from the American Jewish community. People who were absolutely unknown to us sent them a parcel with some very expensive American clothes. Selling that stuff on the black market gave them much needed support.

The atmosphere in Kiev's Jewish families in those days was quite disturbing. Some were thinking that we all had to go, no matter where: Israel, America, Europe, Canada, any place we could, just go. Others were strongly against it arguing that the West sold their Jewish population down the river to the Nazis during the war, but the Soviet Army did everything to protect us and in fact liberated the survivors in Europe. Israel, they worried, may be an even worse trap than Europe. The majority was passively sympathizing with emigration but were too busy to try it on themselves.

Our family was like many others. My sister was emigrating, I was in full support of them, but was not planning myself. Grandpa Solomon, who would object to it, had already passed away. My mother was in full support of the idea but thought that we all should to go together and go to Israel, not America. She took it very hard that she would never see her grandchildren again. My father, under the influence of his older sister Ada, strongly objected at first, but then accepted the fact and helped them with everything he could.

There were endless jokes about the subject; for example, that there is an old Jew sitting at the border-crossing station thinking about something with the expression of big doubt on his face. The border police officer approached him with a question:

"So, old man, you are probably thinking for the last time, should you go or not?"

"No, you idiot," the old man answered, "I am thinking if I should take my umbrella with me."

A note. Remember that the year was 1979, the empire was at full strength, there were no prophets to predict the collapse within a decade. Many could see the worsening economic situation, but considering historical tolerance of Russian people to extreme poverty and hardship, it could easily last another couple hundred years. Therefore, we were all saying goodbye to our friends and our family members forever. The farewell parties looked more like funerals than celebrations of new beginnings.

Chop

Finally, in the late fall of 1979 my sister's family got their permission to leave. Preparations were very fast—you'd want to leave as soon as possible before the authorities changed their minds. They bought train tickets to Vienna, with transfer at the border-crossing station of Chop, which was and still is located where the western Ukraine border meets the Hungarian and Slovakian borders. The family council decided that, having a small kid, they would need help in Chop, so I volunteered to go with them and so did my brother-in-law's older brother Dimitry.

The problem was that the Chop area was a closed border zone and only local residents and travelers with special permits were allowed there. But the Melikha, as usual, underestimated the ingenuity of our people. Some of my friends introduced me to a guy who previously accomplished the mission of accompanying his relatives. The guy gave me very clear instructions and we set off to work.

Dimitry and I bought our tickets to Uzhhorod, taking the same train my sister's family was taking. The train was making a very short stop at the Chop station early in the morning touching, the border and then continuing north to Uzhhorod, an ordinary city in western Ukraine. Since we were buying our tickets to Uzhhorod, it would not raise any suspicions. The guy explained to us that at the Chop station only train cars with the emigres will open the doors, and all other cars would be locked. So, a couple hours before the train was to arrive in Chop, Dimitry and I quietly moved into my sister's car and dissolved into the mess of bags, suitcases, men, women, and children. Everyone knew that the stop would be ridiculously short, so we organized ourselves in such way that when the train approached the station, all women, children, and elderly were accumulated at one end of the car and all the luggage and men at the other. As soon as the train stopped, women and kids started unloading through one door and men stood in a chain and just dumped all the luggage without distinguishing who it belonged to through the other door onto the platform, building an impressive pile. Our help of course was greatly appreciated. The first border patrol showed up, as was predicted, about twenty minutes after the train left the platform. We had just finished sorting out the pile and helping everyone move inside the station's building. The plan was that one of us was supposed to be caught right away and the other should try to hide. So, Dimitry left the station trying to find some milk for our nephew and I was hanging out inside the station. The border patrol was meticulously checking everyone's paperwork and when they approached us, I showed my passport and told them that I was just trying to help my sister to unload the bags onto the platform and that the train left so fast that I just did not have a chance to make it back on. Needless to say, I was immediately detained and taken to the local office for questioning. There I repeated the same b.s. story several times, filled out endless paperwork and repeated it again in writing. I waited for a few hours, I am guessing, for the background check, Finally, I was issued a fee ticket for a first offense with instructions to pay and leave. The key was to delay the payment until the mission was accomplished and my sister's train left the station.

By the time I returned to the station it was close to noon. Not much changed, families were sitting in groups waiting. The train to Vienna was departing in the evening, and the custom check was supposed to start in the late afternoon. I easily found my sister's family. Dimitry was with them. He managed to find some milk for the baby, which actually turned out to be a wasted effort because the custom officers later poured this milk out into the drain under the guise of searching for hidden diamonds. We ended up just hanging around talking all afternoon. All of us realized that we may not see each other ever again, so those few hours were treasured by us all. We knew that the next border patrol sweep would come when the customs check began. This time it would be Dimitry's turn to be detained and I was supposed to talk my way out to stay.

A note. It would be naive to believe that our little tricks were not well-known to the authorities. My guess is that they did tolerate it in limited numbers for several reasons. First, they could single out and collect information they needed about us, the potential troublemakers. Second, in addition to the information, they collected pretty good fees from the fines they had us pay. And third, please see my earlier reference to Ayn Rand about the rules that were meant to be broken.

Around five p.m. the customs circus began. Each family placed their possessions on a flat cart and a local porter pushed this cart through a set of swinging double doors. The carts were full of huge bags and suitcases. I probably need to explain why. Those families were leaving the Soviet Union for permanent settling in Israel. At least this was their official point of destination stated in the documents. Those who were leaving for Israel were allowed to exchange no more than $90 per person, meaning that a family with two children could exchange only that part of their life savings in rubles which corresponded to $360; everything else was left behind. So, people were taking as much as they could carry of the simple things like towels, blankets and so on to avoid having to buy them later upon arrival, since money was so limited. In addition, to have at least some financial cushioning, people were taking with them anything that could possibly be sold in Austria or Italy, the countries that they would pass through on their way. Which of the questionable quality Soviet products could be sold in the West, you may ask? Well, gold and jewelry, photo cameras, some mechanical watches, and vodka. All those objects were restricted and limited. Allowances for the gold and jewelry were very low and should not have historical value. So, even the family rings, earrings, and other heirlooms that were left in the Jewish families after the decades of pogroms, wars, and communist expropriations, were carefully scrutinized by the customs officials and could be rejected at their will. Productions of Soviet industries were allowed for "personal use only," meaning one or two items per person. This included photo cameras, binoculars, and hand watches. Vodka was limited to two half-liter bottles per adult, cigarettes were limited to one block per adult, and so on. The task of the vigilant customs officers was to make sure that the emigres did not hide in their possession any of those items over the allowed limit. Despite the obvious fact that the people were already robbed down to their bones, the crooked Melikha made all efforts to make sure that the emigres felt that they were the offenders and crooks. When we were leaving ten years later, everything was exactly the same, so I will not repeat myself in the later chapters.

To pretend to play fair, when the customs officers deemed some items to be restricted or exceeding the limits, they would go out into the station hall and call the relatives of the departing person with the fake intention of returning the item. They knew well that the station was in the restricted border zone where no relatives were allowed. This was one of the paradoxes that existed but could not be logically explained. To fix the problem on their end, the second border patrol sweep was scheduled right after the custom checks began to make sure those few relatives who managed to escape the first sweep were removed from the station.

This time the border patrol detained about five guys, including my relative Dimitry. I showed my fine ticket to the border patrol officer and explained that I was on my way to pay the fine and just swung by the station to ask someone for the directions to the nearest savings bank. My explanation was accepted as good enough, the officer gave me the directions to the bank and moved on. The detained guys were shouting to me the last names of their families asking for backup while the whole cortège was leaving. After the dust settled, there was only I and one other guy left in the waiting area. We split the duties and each of us walked in several times claiming that we were the relatives. The emigres were nodding, probably trying to guess what was going on, and the customs officers did not object. I received back a bottle of vodka from my sister, a couple more bottles from other families, and, if I remember correctly, an amber necklace or something like that.

When the show was over, I asked my companion to watch the stuff and went to the savings bank to finally pay the fine. I believe that he had already paid his earlier. Walking back, I absolutely unintentionally looked at the railroad station layout and noticed a gap between the station building wall and the parallel neighboring fence forming a tunnel about maybe eight to ten feet wide and about a hundred feet deep. The gap was blocked by a cagelike forged section of a fence, through which I could see some of the platform. A wild thought that I could probably see them boarding the train immediately came to my mind, but I brushed it off.

I came back to the station and was hanging out with my new buddy until the rest of the guys started coming back one-by-one. The items were returned to the corresponding family members, the tickets back home were bought, and there was nothing else for us to do but wait for our trains.

One of the guys looked at his hand watch and sighed that right now they should probably be boarding. The wild thought immediately came back. "Hey, anyone want to see?" I asked.

Everyone did, and I quickly took the group to the forged section I noticed earlier. We leaned our faces against the cold metal. The dusk was already falling and the lights on the platform were on. Through the mist I could see the figures of men pushing their carts passing through the narrow gap of my view and the women holding the hands or carrying their children. I could not distinguish faces, only the silhouettes of their profiles. The picture was sad, but one other detail was shocking. Along the platform there were soldiers standing in a chain between the station building and the platform facing the passing emigres. The soldiers' backs were turned to us. The soldiers were armed with Kalashnikov machine guns. The shocking detail was that the soldiers were holding their guns tilted forward at the ready, pointed at the passing families. I could not believe my eyes! It looked like a bad Nazi movie, but it was true, it was here, right in front of me, I could see a couple of them through the gap. The military I was an officer of, was pointing guns at women and children? At my people's women and children, at my family, at me? I was shocked, thousands of thoughts came rushing through my mind in a split second. Thoughts about Stalin, about the six-day war, about the invasion of Czechoslovakia, about my daughter . . . This was my first big turning point.

A note. Imagine being born in jail. Just a low security jail kind of where you can move more or less freely inside, but with the fence and guard towers around the perimeter. Your parents live in this jail, your grandparents live here. You work all day but have a guaranteed meal three times a day and a plank bed in the barracks. The food is grub but is guaranteed. You would probably accept this life as normal because it's all you know and everyone else around you lives the same. From your early childhood the administration of the prison is constantly telling you how lucky you are to be born here. Because over there, behind that fence, there are swarms of hungry wild people that are sleeping on the streets and are killing each other for food. They even show you some pictures of those people on TV. And those wild people are dreaming of coming here and taking over your place and your food, and your bed. And they would certainly come over and do that, would it not be for the well-protected fence and the brave soldiers in green uniforms standing on the towers day and night keeping you safe. Then imagine that you saw something, something like what I had seen that night, and you have suddenly realized that no, the place I am living in is a prison, that on the other side of the fence is freedom, maybe wild, but freedom, and those guys in their green uniforms are not protecting me from being harmed but are guarding me so that I do not escape. Would not you be shocked?

The whole experience lasted just a few minutes. One of the guys who was with us shouted out the name of his brother, who he probably imagined seeing, and the border patrol showed up almost immediately. This time they were serious. They checked our documents, our receipts from the bank, and our tickets, accompanied us back to the station, and gave us very firm instructions to not leave the station and to depart tonight according to our tickets. Otherwise we would be arrested, and the consequences would be severe. We listened very carefully and nodded our heads, no one wanted to get in trouble.

In the last hour prior to our departure back to Kiev, Dimitry and I, along with a couple of other guys departing on the same train, went to the station cafeteria, got some cold food, cracked a bottle of vodka, and drank "to them," to their success. Then we boarded our train and went to sleep because the next morning all of us had to go to work straight from the train station.

The next day, of course, I told my parents that everything was OK, that they departed, and you should wait for their letters from out there. I only told Tatyana what I saw on the platform, and she was shocked as much as I was. This was when we started talking about the emigrating from the Soviet Union for the first time. Our talks did not last long. In about a week after my return from Chop, Soviet troops invaded Afghanistan and Jewish emigration was halted for almost ten years.

Grandma Lisa

In the summer of 1980 my mother-in-law Tonya was planning to visit her native village in the Yaroslavl region of Russia to see her elderly mother and her younger sister still living there with her family. Our daughter Masha was almost three and we decided that she was big enough for travel, so we decided to come along. Tatyana wanted to show me her birthplace and also to see her grandmother Lisa and her aunties she had not seen for years. Grandma Lisa had never seen me and our daughter, her great granddaughter, so the deal was settled.

We flew to Tula, grabbed Tatyana's mother Tonya and took the train to Yaroslavl. Under normal circumstances we would have to change trains in Moscow, walking from the Kursk railroad station to the Yaroslavl station. But that year the Moscow Olympic Games were in full swing and Moscow was completely locked out for everyone, so our train somehow bypassed the capital and delivered us straight to our destination. We were probably the only ones who benefited from those games.

We spent the first couple days in the city, staying with Tatyana's auntie from her father's side, Vera, whom I had already met at our wedding. Their family lived in the center of the city in the same kind of two-room, about three hundred twenty square feet, government apartment. Amazing how everyone would always find a space for the visiting family or friends despite very limited space.

I liked Yaroslavl, it resembled my Kiev. Both cities were very ancient for Russia, about one and a half millennia old, both lying on the west bank of the big rivers, both very light and breathy, Kiev being a few hundred years older. In fact, the city of Yaroslavl was founded by the duke of Kiev, Yaroslav The Wise, hence the name of the city. I could not compare what I saw there with the dark, grimy, and murky industrial Tula where I lived for five years, though Yaroslavl was no less industrial. Tatyana moved to Tula when she was eight but visited the city often enough to show me the most interesting parts.

A few days later we moved on to continue our journey toward our destination. Grandma's village Duboviky was located on the other side of the Volga River deeper inland. We took an early morning bus that crossed the river bridge and then continued for quite a while until Tonya requested the stop and the bus driver dropped us in the middle of nowhere at the intersection of some paved and unpaved roads. The bus continued along the paved road eastward and we began walking on the unpaved one northward. Tonya and Tatyana explained to me that there are four villages along this branch, Duboviky being the last about five kilometers away. When I asked what is beyond it, if the road ends, they could not answer clearly. "The wild forest," they said, "for many kilometers."

A linguistic note. Dub in Russian means oak tree, so the village name Duboviky is analogous to Oakville in English.

There we went, carrying all our suitcases and gifts along that unpaved, uneven dirt road, feeling lucky that there was no rain because mud would make it impassable. Three-year-old Masha heroically walked for about half a kilometer and then I had to carry her in my arms. Somewhere halfway we met a man on a tractor with a trailer who recognized Tonya and gave us a highly appreciated ride for a few kilometers to the village of Dor. The last stretch from Dor to Duboviky we walked again. When we crossed a small creek both women got excited telling me that the destination was near.

The village was small, fourteen households. Twelve of them shared the same last name, Alaev. This was also the maiden name of Tatyana's mother. Behind the village was a winding little river It', a tributary of the Volga. Behind the river was that large forest that they talked about, we later went there a few times to pick some wild berries and mushrooms.

The houses were made from logs, plastered inside, but looking natural from outside. There was no running water, but every household had a well. Conveniences were outdoors. Because of the cold climate, the houses were built around a huge, wood-burning, brick stove, which served for both cooking and heating. The mouth of the stove was in the kitchen, but each room in the house shared one brick wall with that stove. There was also a summer room, called "gornitsa." Entering the house through the covered porch, or veranda, straight ahead was the summer room, to the right were the living quarters with the stove in the middle, and to the left was the barn where the livestock was held, all under the same roof. The toilet was between the summer room and the barn. Though not heated, it was still inside the structure, so that you did not have to fight the cold and snow to go to the outhouse. As an engineer I was amazed how rationally everything was built.

Our hosts were grandma Lisa, auntie Julia, Julia's husband Pavel, and their teenage daughter Nadia. They also had an older, son, Vadim who was already married and lived somewhere else. Julia and Pavel were working at the collective farm, so we saw them only in the evenings, and Nadia hung around with us and showed us around. Grandma was already eighty-six, she barely moved, but you could tell right away that she was in charge.

Another family member was a she-cat, Muska, a very interesting character. She was very independent and pretty mean, enough to say that the local dogs were afraid to mess with her. When we walked in, she smelled every one of us very carefully, paying special attention to our daughter Masha. After that, she allowed Masha to play with her, and Tatyana and I were completely ignored. Her favorite family member was auntie Julia, who worked at the milk farm in the Dor, the village we passed by on our way to Duboviky. Every morning before the sunrise, still in the dark, the cat accompanied Julia on her way to work as far as the creek, and then disappeared, going about her cat business. When Julia was coming back from work, the cat waited for her at the same spot near the creek and accompanied her back home. It did not matter what time Julia was coming home, early or late, the cat was always there. Grandma used to say: "Look, the cat is out, Julia will be home in a few minutes."

The family treated me very well, but I could feel that I was a foreigner in their eyes, especially in the beginning. They would treat an American or a Martian about the same way.

Probably the second day there, we were sitting around the dinner table and I asked grandma about the old times, how was their life here before the revolution. I was just curious. With the influence of my new co-workers, my trip to Chop, the letters from my sister in America, and continuous thinking and analysis, I started having big doubts in my mind about the truthfulness and correctness of the information we were receiving at our schools and colleges about our own history. Here I had a perfect opportunity to talk to a living witness. All my grandparents were already gone and a stranger, even if I could find one still alive, would probably be afraid to tell me the truth. I did not start this conversation intentionally, it just happened that we started talking about it. Grandma's stories were shocking. Tatyana and I just looked at each other and asked her to please continue. I guess no one had asked her about those past events for years; the family was probably too busy with their hard work and everyday challenges, or they just were not interested.

Grandma, on the other hand, when met with the appreciative listeners, started telling us more and more stories, remembering something new every day. We would sit with her for hours just listening. Unfortunately, I did not write down her stories at the time, almost forty years ago, but in essence she told us that before the revolution life was much better and merrier. When she was growing up, her family lived in a big house and owned some land that they worked and lived off. In addition, her father, Efrem, had a convenience store which also brought some cash to the family budget. The money for the store came from Efrem's older brother who served in the tsar's military and received some money when he was discharged (this reminds me of my great-grandfather's story and his mill). The brother became a merchant and got wealthy enough to help Efrem.

"Ok," I asked Grandma, "not everyone had a store, how did the other people in the village live?"

"Everyone who was willing to work lived well," was the answer. "Only the lazy and the drunk were poor. By the way," she continued, "those lazy and drunk, and later their children, rose up with the revolution and became the local party bosses."

Once she told us a story about the local landlord, "barin" in Russian. The history lessons in school told us that the landlord would force the farmers to work on his land for free. Grandma told us that they actually worked on his land for cash. Moreover, for the local youth it was the only source of cash because otherwise they were working on their family farms and the cash was in the hands of their parents. So, the crop gathering for the landlord was always concluded with a massive youth party in the evening with songs and dances and love adventures. "I could not go there anymore after I got married," grandma told us, laughing. "Very disappointing." She also told us that during the Civil War while the landlord was away fighting, the local peasants would hide his wife and kids from the Bolsheviks.

"Grandma, but what happened then, during the revolution?"

"Then those villains and bastards came in and took everything!"

"Grandma who? The Whites?"

"No, the Reds!"

A historical note. At this point I owe my American reader a brief tour into the history of the Russian Revolution and Civil War. Everyone has probably heard some information about the Russian Revolution in October of 1917. But not everyone knows that actually there were two revolutions happening in Russia that year. The first revolution took place in February, starting as a hunger riot in Petrograd (now St. Petersburg, former Leningrad) and ending with abdication of Tsar Nicholas II when the local military garrison joined the mutiny. The revolution was accidental, absolutely not planned, and without any leadership. The progressively minded Russian intelligentsia formed a Provisional Government and started working on establishing at least some democratic institutions in the huge belligerent country that had been under autocratic rule since antiquity. This first event is called the Bourgeois Revolution in Russian historiography. If it would have stopped there, the present for the Russian people would probably be much brighter. Unfortunately, it did not.

The Bolsheviks, a small group of extreme radicals, saw the opportunity and organized another revolution, practically a coup, in October of the same year. Their agitators penetrated the Petrograd navy base and convinced with their radical rhetoric the navy sailors to join the coup. The sailors brought a navy ship along the Neva River right up to the palace where the Provisional Government was working and opened fire from heavy artillery guns. The mutineers stormed the palace that had very few guards and overthrew the government, declaring the Dictatorship of the Proletariat in the whole country. That second event is called the Socialist Revolution in Russian historiography.

I've heard the opinion that the October revolution was pulled off by drunk sailors. Well, to make a sailor drunk somebody has to buy him a drink. I will not drag this narrative into conspiracy theories, but the most prevailing opinion is that the coup was financed by the German General Command with intent to take Russia out of the World War I without firing a shot.

In any case, the things went from bad to worse and then to catastrophic. Facing the coup, Russia's democratically leaning intelligentsia and the military officers joined in the opposition to the new regime, calling it the White Movement and forming the opposition military force called the White Guard, or in simple terms The Whites. The Bolsheviks, facing an opposition from the military, formed their own new

armed forces, called the Red Army, or in simple terms
The Reds. This started the Russian Civil War.

The White Movement was a loose affiliation of
motley groups from monarchists to social democrats
without any unifying program or idea. They knew
exactly what they were against but could not show
what they were for. The Bolsheviks, on the other hand,
offered three simple slogans: Factories to the Workers,
Land to the Farmers, and Peace to the People! This was
enough to unify the working class, the peasants, and
even some intelligentsia. As the result of those simple
slogans the Bolsheviks won.

The problem is that ruling the country for
seventy years, the Bolsheviks did not fulfill any of those
promises. The factories were controlled by the
Communist elite, the land was grabbed from the
farmers during the collectivization and never returned,
and during the Bolsheviks' rule there was never peace
in the land. This is why I tell the young generation: Do
not believe anyone who calls for taking from the rich
and giving to the poor! They may take it from the rich
all right, but will never give it to the poor. They will
keep it for themselves, forming a new elite.

In Ukraine, by the way, the situation was even
more complex during the Civil War, with Ukrainian
nationalists fighting for independence, German
military occupying half the country including Kiev,
and a bunch of anarchist groups controlling significant
territories in the southeast. All of these groups,
including the Reds and the Whites, committed bloody
pogroms against the Jewish population, except for the

Germans. With very limited choices, most Jews were leaning towards Bolsheviks who were promising equality for all, and joined the Red Army. They were not allowed to form their own Jewish units for self-defense and instead were spread between overwhelmingly larger Ukrainian and Russian populaces, which kept them helpless.

Going back to the grandma. She was not glorifying the tsarist regime, she just told us how much worse it became during the Revolution and the Civil War. The White Army never came even close to their region, but the kids of the local "lazy and drunk" immediately joined the Bolsheviks and became their representatives. Grandma even gave us the names of those people, but it is irrelevant now. Those people practically declared a war on the local farmers, taking revenge for the past. Her father Efrem, for example, was dragged several times by the beard across the village to be executed and saved his life only by giving away all his life savings earned with hard labor over the years. And he was not the only one.

Grandma Lisa was already married with two children and her husband away in the army. The villains, as she called them, came to her several times taking everything they could find. One winter, she told us, she saved a few sacks of grain from the last harvest in hope to feed the children. Accidentally she found out from her sources that they were coming that day. So, she harnessed horse into the sled, hid those couple sacks in the sled under some coats and went driving through the village, telling everyone she met that she was going to visit her sister in the neighboring village. Once she was in the forest, she spotted a couple places she would be able to recognize later and, without stopping the horse, threw the sacks out into the snow as far as she could. "Why without stopping?" we asked. "Because when they follow, they could easily see where the horse stopped by the tracks in the snow and would have found the sacks." A couple days later, after the "villains and bastards" left, Lisa came back and retrieved the sacks. This was the extent of revolutionary expropriation from the bourgeoisie.

Grandma Lisa told us a lot of stories during the week that we stayed with her, but we knew that she still did not tell us everything. For example, she told us that during the Civil War her husband Alexander sent her letters from Crimea calling her to grab the kids and come over. Up to then she still regretted that she did not. But it is a well-known fact that the Crimea was a territory controlled by the White Guard. "So, was grandpa serving with the Whites?" we asked. "How do I know," she answered, "the men were fighting somewhere, we did not even know where," and changed the subject. If we guessed it correctly, had she gone to Crimea back then, Tatyana's mother would be probably born somewhere in

Paris . . . This is where the leftovers of the White Guard ended up after their defeat.

Grandma's past was and now will forever remain an enigma. For example, she told us that when the villains came, she burned all her documents. Why? We had noticed that she was literate—and not just literate, her mathematical skills were also impressive, which was very unusual for the environment she claimed to have grown up in. She had two different maiden last names in different documents. Why, if Efrem's last name was well-known to everyone? And so on.

Grandma Lisa's stories finished the job of my eye-opening. First, she confirmed my suspicions that the history they were teaching us was a lie. Logically, if their history lessons were a lie, then everything else they were telling us must be a lie. But the most important outcome of my talks with Tatyana's grandma was that I started realizing that my Jewishness was not my primary problem. The problem was not with me or with Grandma Lisa, or with my grandfather Zelik. The problem was with the SYSTEM. And, since I could not change the system, the only solution was to grab my wife and my daughter and get out of there. As soon as possible, as fast as possible, and as far as possible.

Life on Hold

An advertisement in the newspaper: "Will buy one linear meter of the State Border Line"
(A Jewish joke in the early 1980s.)

OK, now when the decision was made, the next logical step ought to have been the execution. In our case, the gap between the decision and the execution was nine years, an eternity in human life. In 1980, when we came back from that Yaroslavl vacation, Brezhnev was still in power, the Soviet troops were still in Afghanistan, the Olympic Games were boycotted, the borders were closed, and emigration was nullified. On top of all these external challenges, we had a pretty big internal challenge. Though Tatyana was theoretically agreeing with me that we must go, she had parents and no siblings to take care of them. If we left, she would never see her parents again, there would be no one to take care of them when they got older, no one to bury them if G-d forbid something happened. But at that point, since we could not do anything anyway, we just put this problem on the back burner to resolve later.

In 1981 my mother passed away from a heart attack; she was only 53. A year later my father married another woman, Rita, who was his sweetheart before he met my mother. Of course, I did not know she existed and was surprised and a little jealous. Rita left her husband with whom she was obviously unhappy to marry my dad. She had a daughter exactly my age, so I unexpectedly got a sister. Rita's family lived in Rostov, so she moved to Kiev to live with my dad. They stayed in Kiev for a little while and then moved to Kislovodsk, a little resort city in the foothills of the Caucasus mountains, leaving us my father's apartment.

I changed a couple of jobs, ending up at a high-voltage startup engineering office with the Ministry of Agriculture Machinery. My good friend, an electrical engineer, invited me there. At that time the wiseguys in the Kremlin decided that in order to resolve the food shortage in the country, they had to mechanize the agricultural production (instead of disbanding the collective farms and giving the land back to the farmers). They started building multiple agricultural machinery production plants all over Ukraine and Moldova and our office was providing testing and startup services for electrical power distribution substations at those plants. The work involved heavy travel, two to three weeks a month away from home, but better pay.

Sometime during this period we noticed that we were under surveillance. First of all, Tatyana was complaining that someone was following her several times on her way home from work. I had not noticed anything, but women feel this kind of thing much better than men. And then two of our neighbor ladies told me that there were some men who had approached them a couple times and asked about me. Those were retired elderly women from our apartment section who were customarily sitting on the bench near the entry porch chatting about their women things (and of course about everyone who enters and exits the door) after all their household chores were completed. By the way, having these constant security guards on hand, nobody was afraid to leave kids playing alone in the apartment courtyard. Anyway, these ladies had known me since I was a little kid and told me about this surveillance right away. Maybe this was a consequence of my trip to Chop, maybe not, who knows? I'd love to peek into my KGB file . . .

But life went on. We always wanted to have a second baby but were putting it on hold because of our emigration plans. In 1984 one of Tatyana's friends had a boy. Looking at this baby Tatyana was done waiting and in 1985 gave birth to our son Boris.

Boris was born in the Central Maternity Hospital on Shevchenko Boulevard in Kiev, a pretty elite place, but since Tatyana was working in the Medical Institute, she was able to prearrange that place for herself. The preparations for giving birth were a little different back then. The day she felt that she was going into labor I managed to be home. We got on a public trolley-bus and all three of us went to the hospital; we could not leave Masha home alone, so she went with us. Tatyana said that it was not urgent, otherwise we would have taken a taxi. As most families back then, we did not have a car. It just happened that that day there was some roadwork near the hospital and we had to walk the last few city blocks being mad at ourselves for not taking a taxi. On our way to the hospital we met some friends and stopped to chat until Tatyana said that we'd better go now, it's really time. Masha and I took her to the doors, and that was it. She walked in and we had to stay outside. No one, except the women in childbirth, were allowed inside for the sake of sterility. And it was also believed that the men had nothing to do there anyway. That night around 11p.m. the nurse called me at home and congratulated me on the birth of my son. I forgot to mention that we did not know the gender until the baby was born, as the technology had not been developed yet.

The post-maternity room, according to Tatyana, looked more like a military barracks with ten beds in one big room where the confined mothers were staying. That hospital was distinguished by having a common shower, while the other hospitals did not have shower at all. Masha and I visited them a couple times, but the visits were limited to standing on the street under the window of her room and yelling in hope that she would hear us and look out the window. You can imagine that we had a good company of other young men, some with kids, standing there and yelling next to us, giving everyone that feeling of a comradery. If everything was OK with the mom and the baby, women were usually released after approximately seven days. Since it was her second baby, Tatyana was out in five.

In relation to this story, the day after Boris was born, I stopped at the little cafe to have a cup of coffee and, while standing in line, overheard a conversation of some guys behind me discussing how drunk they had gotten the day before celebrating Passover. The Russian language has the same word for both the Jewish Passover and the Christian Easter. I turned around and looked at their faces—members of the tribe, it was OK to talk.

"What Passover, Jewish Passover?"

"Yes, did you not know yesterday was Jewish Passover!"

"Wow, what a coincidence, my son was born yesterday!"

"Congrats, dude," and they continued their talks.

Needless to tell my reader that we did not follow many Jewish Holidays those days and even

120

if we did (like those guys behind me) it was way different from the orthodox ways. I was usually trying to at least keep track of the major ones, but that year I understandably was too busy and missed it.

However, the revelation I received that morning drinking my cup of coffee was astounding. So, my son was born on the first night of Passover! This is it, this must be a sign! He will take us out of here!

Well, everyone believes what he chooses to believe, but something snapped inside of me that morning and I was back in the game. Not sure though why it took Boris so long, the whole four years, to fulfill his mission. Maybe he just needed to learn how to walk before taking us out of there.

But seriously, the situation in the country was changing rapidly. After the death of Brezhnev in November 1982, the new guy, former KGB head Andropov ruled for only fifteen months and died in February 1984. After him the Party appointed this old dude Chernenko, who could barely move and died one year later in March of 1985. In April of 1985, when Boris was born, yet another new leader was just appointed. This time it was the relatively young and ambitious Mikhail Gorbachev, who was also connected to the KGB and was considered the follower of Andropov's hard line. Here, in the West, Gorbachev for some reason has a reputation of a reformer, maybe because of his Perestroika program. "Perestroika" in Russian means simply a "re-building" or "re-construction." The purpose of his program was not the reformation of the system, but the preservation of the collapsing system. Maybe in the West it looked like a new revelation, but for us, living inside the system and seeing so many "constructions" and "re-constructions" before, it was just another bunch of propaganda b.s. The economy was getting worse and worse, life tougher and tougher, food less and less available. The collapse of the Soviet Union six years later was already predetermined and probably even pre-scheduled, it's just that nobody knew about it yet. All Gorbachev's preservation reforms were in vain, doomed to fail. Pardon my vulgar analogy, but it was like curing diarrhea by plugging an a-hole with a cork. His only achievement was maybe slightly impeding the process of the collapse, if the collapse could be impeded at all.

Major catastrophes were happening during his rule, one after another. In Kiev people were openly talking about the Egyptian plagues and we know that the people's wisdom rarely is wrong. One of those plagues was Chernobyl.

The Plague

The town of Chernobyl lies about 130 kilometers (81 miles) north from Kiev. The accident at the Chernobyl nuclear plant happened on Saturday, April 26, 1986, a few days before the First of May holidays and the long weekend. At the beginning the Melikha did not tell us anything about what happened, as usual trying to hide its own mishaps. If it was not for the wind blowing toward Northern Europe that day, the world would have never known about the Chernobyl catastrophe. The population was not evacuated, the forced pro-Communist parade proceeded through downtown, children were playing in the streets, and so on. May 1st and 2nd were two holidays followed by Saturday and Sunday. My father was visiting us from Kislovodsk and on Friday, May 2nd, we took our nine-year-old Masha across the city to the cemetery for a spring cleanup of my mother's grave. I have to admit that there were rumors going around the city about some horrible industrial accident happening somewhere, but there were so many different rumors floating around all the time, due to the lack of information, that we did not really pay attention to any of them.

Saturday morning, it was already May 3rd, I went out to buy some milk for our one-year-old baby Boris. The easiest way was to buy milk from the large metal thermo-insulated barrels set on wheels as a trailer and stationed in the morning at certain known street corners. You would have to bring your own vessel and the saleswoman would fill it from the tap, just like beer. Actually, the beer was sold in a similar way. Anyway, I went to the usual street corner that morning, but the milk barrel was not there. OK, I thought, maybe I am too late, and they already sold the milk. I went to the nearest grocery store to buy bottled milk, but there was no milk on the shelves. Well, I thought, looks like we are getting a new deficit item, milk, I better go and buy a dry milk powder before it's too late. It is hard to explain, but in the Soviet Union different kind of products were appearing in different stores. I knew of one place in downtown where I always saw shelves full of boxes of dry milk. So, I took the trolley-bus and went to that store. All the shelves were empty!

My mind immediately pulled out from my memory old information received during my college military training. During the nuclear war, we were taught, milk is one of the first products to become radioactive. Even if a small concentration radioactive cloud falls on the grass and a cow eats that grass, the milk becomes radioactive. We, as officers, were told to make sure that our troops did not drink the milk from cows near the zone of a nuclear strike. With the rumors and that knowledge combined came a realization that hit me like a lightning bolt. I found a taxi and raced home. Quickly explaining what happened, we decided that Tatyana and Boris must immediately fly to Tula to her parents. My father was planning to take Masha with him to Kislovodsk for the summer vacation anyway, they already had tickets for May 10 (a week from the date) we were just waiting for the end of the school year. I grabbed the money and Tatyana's passport and took the taxi again to the Aeroflot ticket office downtown. When I ran into the ticket office, there was still no line and I bought airplane tickets for the next morning's flight. That afternoon panic hit the city. The lines in all ticket offices built up for several city blocks, people were spending nights in those lines trying to send their loved ones away.

A note. This example shows once again that there is no such thing as useless information. At some point in life any information may become very useful.

My big mistake was that I did not also send Masha with them to Tula because events started unfolding in an avalanche. That Sunday when Tatyana left, the Chernobyl incident was finally officially announced. It was not because the

125

Melikha was trying to save its own people, but because the radiation cloud hit Western and Northern Europe and they could not hide it any longer. Would the wind have blown southeast that week, a few thousand people would mysteriously have died in Kiev or somewhere else, and nobody would ever have known why. They would probably find a way to blame it on the imperialists and Zionists.

But fortunately for us and unfortunately for the northern regions, the wind was blowing North, away from Kiev. The accident was announced, but we were told that the radiation level was within the norm and that our caring government was just taking precautionary measures. Later we found out that the "norm," the officially acceptable radiation contamination level, was increased tenfold that day to make the level fit within the norm. Simple and elegant.

The next day, when I took our daughter to school, I was told that the schools were closed for early summer break and that it was recommended that all children be taken out of the city. If we were not able to take her out of the city, our loving government would organize special summer camps and I could give my daughter to this camp. So, now it was forced evacuation of the children, and I could have sent her away with her mother two days ago, what an idiot!

At this point it was practically impossible to buy or exchange any tickets. My father's train was in five days and we had no other option than to wait. I was between my business trips and was supposed to go back to work the week my father and daughter were leaving, this was how we pre-scheduled it. For the next couple days, we just watched the news and watched the city emptying out; the women and children were leaving. At that moment I was not in panic yet, I knew enough to see that no one around me died, and no one was getting sick. As a precautionary measure we were not leaving home without necessity. I realized that we may receive a low dose of radiation, but if Masha got out in a few days, she would still be OK. All the remaining population in Kiev became experts in the radiation sciences, we were following the numbers and buying selected products and food. Our biggest concern was water. The majority of the water supply in Kiev comes from the Dnieper river, which flows from north to south. Chernobyl is situated upstream, in the north. Even with the northern wind and limited contamination of the soil, the water was coming straight from the place of the accident and could be dangerous. The official levels of water contamination given to us on TV were within the norm, but who would believe them after what had happened? We were trying to drink only bottled water and limited our showers.

Everything was good until one evening, two days before my father and daughter's departure date, I met with my good friend who was a math teacher in one of the city's most elite high schools. Through the parents of his students, he had access to much better information than I was receiving watching TV. My friend told me that the sarcophagus they were trying to build around the reactor was not working, and that they were considering an option of setting up a cumulative explosion to bury the whole reactor under the ground. I knew a little bit about explosions from my mining studies. Actually, this was technically possible, hence it sounded realistic, but very dangerous. Remember that the essence of the whole Chernobyl accident was the release of the heavy water steam from the cooling jacket into the atmosphere and the reactor's core overheating and melting down. The reactor itself had never exploded. Now, if they were setting a controlled explosion and something went wrong, the reactor itself may explode and the situation would become much worse than it originally was. They could have botched it easily. If the engineers could be left alone, they could have probably pulled it off, but I knew who would manage the project. The orders from Moscow and Kiev would botch it for sure.

That was the moment when I started to panic and was panicking for two days straight until I took my daughter and father to the railroad station and sent them away. My only hope was that the preparations for such an action would take a few days and my daughter may have enough time to escape.

The controlled explosion to bury the reactor never happened. The sarcophagus was finished and, though occasionally leaking, is still there. Many years later I read somewhere that the explosion option was in fact considered but was rejected.

The rest of the story is not that exciting. Masha spent summer with my dad, Tatyana and Boris with her parents. I was working alone with the rest of the men in the city, visiting Tatyana a few times. In late August, closer to the beginning of the next school year, the same friend of mine somehow through his connections got a Geiger counter for one day and we checked his and my apartments for radiation levels, both were clean, and our families came back. The city looked weird the whole summer without the children and everyone was happy to see them again. I remember when the first kids started showing up on the streets or public buses, people were giving them sweets and candies.

A note. Five years later, when we were already in the United States, I was working with General Electric and was assigned to do some work in the Vallecitos nuclear power plant in California. The policy required checking every person's radiation level before entering and after exiting the plant to keep a record of received and accumulated dose. My level before entering was zero. *This means that I had not received any radiation dose during the Chernobyl accident because the half-life of Cesium-137, the dominating isotope that was released, is 30 years.*

The Lion's Mark

This chapter is about my glorious military career. As I was mentioning earlier, I graduated from my Institute military department in 1978 in the rank of Lieutenant of Engineering Troops in Reserve. The engineering troops in Russia were more commonly called sappers. In the fall of 1987 I was already in the rank of senior lieutenant in reserve. Twice during those nine years I went through military re-training and two times managed to avoid it. Once I received a call-up notice in the mail one week before our family vacation and to dodge it I just had to exchange the tickets and go on vacation a week earlier and pretend it was lost in the mail. Another time I convinced an officer at the assembly place, the Military Commissariat, to let me go, buying him a bottle of vodka as a bribe. Two other times I was forced to drag my butt after work to the other side of the city for two weeks, being grateful that it was not the military camps. As the result of those two trainings, I was promoted to the next rank.

Now I have to explain to my reader the game of military trainings in the Soviet Army. The service was not voluntary, it was forced. The servicemen were not paid, except for active-duty officers. If you were called from reserve to the camps for a few months, the office you were working at as a civilian was obligated to pay you your average salary. That meant of course that the guys from your office had to cover your duties without additional pay. The conditions in the army were marginal, the food was horrible, and patriotism in the country at that time was at a freezing point. Naturally, everyone was trying to avoid it as much as possible. Nobody was taking seriously the notice in the mail, considering it more like an early warning because one could always claim he had never received it. The Military Commissariat knew about this and, when they really needed more people, were sending messengers to deliver the summons papers to your residence and requesting a signature on the delivery receipt.

That day in September of 1987 was the weekend of Masha's birthday, and we were expecting guests. The doorbell rang, I opened the door, and . . . bang, got the subpoena right in my face!

When I showed up, the officer at the Military Commissariat explained to me that they were preparing me to be a platoon commander in the rank of captain and I must go for additional training, which would take place at the military school in Kaliningrad. I had big doubts when he was trying to assure me that it would only take two to three weeks and I was right, it actually took a full eight weeks. Well, I had no choice.

Unlike the soldiers who traveled in accompanied groups from the Military Commissariat, the officers got to travel on their own. I just had to report to a destination place on a certain date. At the Commissariat they gave me some money for the train ticket and even some per diem for the day of travel. The officer also informed me that I was not the only one sent from Kiev, that there were three other guys from different districts going there too and recommended that we all get together. He gave me their names and telephone numbers.

The departure date was a few weeks away, so we had enough time to call each other and plan the trip together. Kaliningrad is a Russian enclave on the Baltic Sea, squeezed in between Poland and the then-Soviet Baltic Republic, now the independent state of Lithuania. The region, also known as Königsberg, was annexed by the Soviet Union from Germany as a reparation after WWII. There was no direct train from Kiev to Kaliningrad. We had to take an overnight train to Lithuanian capital Vilnius and then travel a few hours on a suburban train to the destination. The plan seemed to be perfectly lined-up. Our train was to arrive at Vilnius early in the morning, and we did not have to report to the military school before the evening, so we could spend a good part of the day exploring Vilnius, where none of us had been before.

On the train I met my new companions, Victor, Vlad, and Andrei, and our seats were together. The guys were ordinary engineers from Kiev, just like me. Andrei was from the Russian Far East, his father as a military officer was at some point transferred to Ukraine and they settled in Kiev. The other two were typical local Kiev homies, and we all became friends very quickly.

Well, the story would be boring if one of the guys did not pull out a bottle of vodka to celebrate our new friendship. Everyone had some food from home with them, so we drank vodka, ate and talked for the rest of the evening. Events started derailing when the guys started talking about getting a second bottle. Evil is always sitting at the bottom of an empty bottle somewhere next to the Truth. Since I was never a big drinker, I told my new friends that I'd pass on the second one and went to sleep. They did not object. Remember, I had two kids at home, one of them two years old. Sleeping for me was no less fun than vodka.

The last thing I heard falling asleep was them discussing the options of where and how to get the second one. Apparently, they succeeded because when the train started approaching Vilnius early the next morning my friends were looking a little out of shape. They jumped up and started excitedly discussing something obviously related to the last night's adventures. From the context I understood that they had some dispute with the conductor woman and now we better exit through the adjacent car. OK, we grabbed our bags and moved along the moving train a few cars away before the train stopped. Successfully debarking on the platform, the guys told me that last night they bought another bottle—this time it was moonshine—from that conductor woman. Then, they told me, the bitch started picking on them, which ended up in a little dispute and her promise to call local police (the militia in Russia), but now we were out, and everything was going to be all right.

Walking down the platform toward the station building, we suddenly saw a policeman running in the opposite direction, toward the train. When he saw the four of us he slowed down and very nicely asked us where we came from, in pretty clear Russian with a noticeable Baltic accent. We replied that we were from Kiev on our way to the military service in Kaliningrad. He became excited and asked us if we wouldn't mind helping him to detain a group of hooligans because he was alone and there should be three of them. We nodded with a mix of caution and enthusiasm, worry and hope. Turning around we followed the guy toward the train, with worry gradually increasing and hope gradually decreasing, as we were approaching the train car we just came from. The conductor lady, of course, was in a state of complete confusion when she saw us coming with the policeman to arrest ourselves. The policeman, looking at her face, started slowly realizing his mistake, as we were vigilantly gazing around pretending to be looking for those hooligans. The situation was as funny as it was awkward. The guy smiled and told us to follow him into the station office. In the office he told his partner something in Lithuanian and they both started laughing, it was most likely about us.

And then something unimaginable happened. The Lithuanian police officers offered us to sit down and one of them asked:

"Did you guys really kick the ass of a Russian policeman on the train?"

I looked at my partners in perplexity, as I not heard anything about the policeman being involved. The guys were sitting silently, staring at the ceiling.

"But he probably started it," continued the officer, "and you were just defending yourselves from his aggression?"

My friends' faces slightly revived.

"I'll tell you what," said the officer, "you Ukrainians live under Russian occupation the same way we Lithuanians live. I am glad that you kicked some Russian ass and I will let you go. Just be careful next time."

And that was the miraculous ending of that story. We flew out of the station police office and were free until that evening. This was the first sign of the empire collapsing that I saw on that trip, the others were to follow. But at that moment none of us paid any attention to those signs, it just felt weird.

A note. The Lithuanian officer obviously had problems with geography. Our train never touched Russian territory, crossing through Belarus straight into Lithuania, so the policeman my friends had quarreled with was most likely a Belarus. Plus, to be precise, only two in our group were Ukrainians; I was Jewish, and Andrei was Russian.

The campus of the military engineering school in Kaliningrad that we had to report to was a campus of an old German military tank school. The buildings were built stoutly with thick red brick walls. The plaza was cobblestone-paved, with heavy, cast-iron utility covers with some texts casted on them in German. This pavement survived German tanks and all kinds of Russian heavy engineering equipment without ever being repaired. In one of those red brick buildings on the second floor were our barracks. It was a huge hall with beds and small nightstands next to the beds, the same setup I had in my college dorm, but on a larger scale. At the entrance was a big table with a bunch of a hard-seated chairs and a TV. After checking in, each of us was issued a uniform with three small stars on our shoulder straps, since all of us were of the same military rank, and we became part of the forces.

A note. The reserve officers in training did not wear the same uniform as the enlisted officers. Our uniform was a leftover from the WWII warehouses—if anyone has seen documentaries from those times, this is what we were wearing and how we looked. The uniform included the flared breeches, the high boots with the foot bindings instead of socks, the soldier's blouse girded with a belt, and of course a trench coat because it was already late fall. Because of this distinguishing uniform the reserve officers were often called "Partisans."

There were groups of guys from different regions of the country. Naturally everyone was trying to hang out with his own group, and our group picked four beds next to each other. The largest group was from Russia, but for me they were like my own after living for five years in Tula. My Ukrainian friends at that time did not have any nationalistic motives yet, so our group naturally blended with the Russian group. But it was not true for everyone. The group from the Baltic Republics—Lithuania, Latvia, and Estonia, was the second in number and they kept themselves completely separated from us, speaking their own languages and communicating with each other but demonstratively avoiding us. I am talking about leisure time—they had to speak Russian in classes, of course. This was the second sign of the empire falling apart; remember that we were not just a bunch of guys, we were military officers in service.

The third shocking sign was how the senior officers, our instructors, most of them in the ranks of colonel or lieutenant colonel, spoke of the current party leader Gorbachev and his government. It was more than just criticism (which itself was unheard of within the military), it was open contempt shown publicly in the classrooms during the lectures. We were laughing, but honestly, I was feeling a little uncomfortable out of habit.

We were studying six days a week with Sunday off. The food was a little better than the soldiers' ration, but still mostly barley kasha and pork fat. In the officer's pieces of fat, however, you could occasionally find some strips of meat.

Morning trooping was funny. We would all line up in formation on the plaza before marching to our classes—cadets in their uniform, us partisans, in our uniform, plus a group of foreign cadets, mostly from Arab and African countries, each in their own uniforms in one joined formation. This looked very odd and funny from a military standpoint, especially when they were marching each in their own rhythm. Once, the instructor gave us some handouts and then, after looking at it, pulled them back saying that these handouts were for the foreigners. When someone asked out of curiosity what was the difference, the instructor explained to us that the foreigners do not receive the complete information. "We teach them only what they paid for. Less they know, easier will be for us to fight against them later." A very simple and practical approach. I must note here that we were kept completely isolated from both the cadets and the foreigners, except for those morning troopings.

I enjoyed the studying. Besides technical updates, they were teaching us leadership skills, basically management courses, knowledge I successfully used later in the United States when I became a manager. One evening after classes one of our curator officers walked into our barracks and asked if anyone could fix the printer. Most of the guys were civil or mining engineers and knew nothing about the printers. Neither did I, but working with electrical startups I volunteered to look at it. The next morning, I was excused from classes and was taken straight into the office. The printing machines in the Soviet Union were considered strategic objects with very limited access. I guess the Melikha was afraid of reprinting samizdat (underground publications) or some prohibited flyers. Therefore, I knew very little about printers, but fixed it within about an hour. I do not remember what specifically I did, probably cleaned the paper jam and restarted. For my superiors it was a miracle and they did not let me go back to my classes for couple days, giving me the assignment of watching a perfectly working printer, just in case. Then, after a few days, realizing how bored I was, they let me go and said that I did not have to show up for the final exam because I would be passing automatically. That was very nice of them, but to their surprise I showed up for the finals. I always liked action; much more fun than sitting in the empty barracks.

In this military school I had another very interesting encounter that I still remember, and that was another shocking sign of the collapsing empire. This time it was with the group from the Caucasian region. One guy in the group was Azerbaijani, the other two were Armenians. For reference, Azerbaijanis are Muslims, Armenians are Christian, and they were adversaries for centuries. The Azerbaijani guy was always alone and rarely talked to anyone. He spoke very limited Russian and, looking at his class performance, I had doubts that he had ever studied anywhere. The Armenian guys were always hanging out together, but their relationships looked a little odd: One of them seemed to be like a servant to the other, though they were about the same age and of the same rank. One evening after school we were hanging out outside the barracks and the "master" came to me and pulled me out to talk. He introduced himself as Ashot and introduced his partner, too, but I do not remember the partner's name. The partner was with us the entire time, but never said a word. I introduced myself. Ashot immediately asked me about my nationality, mentioning that my last name did not sound Russian. I told him that I am Jewish. "This is what I thought," he replied. And then out of the blue he said:

"Do you know that we have a common enemy?" He nodded at the Azerbaijani.

"Well, he is not my enemy," I replied, "but I am getting where you are going."

From the beginning the conversation drifted into a very interesting direction. I found out from Ashot that both he and his partner were not from Armenia, but from Nagorno-Karabakh, an Armenian enclave in Azerbaijan. This gave me at least some logical clue of his defiance of Azerbaijani. Ashot was well-spoken with pretty good and clear Russian, and communication with him was pleasant. We talked that night for about half an hour, and he asked about me and my attitude toward Israel. I was careful not to say too much, but was pretty open, since those two guys did not look like KGB informants. I cannot say that we became friends, because I did not believe a word of what he was saying, but we would hang out together often. His partner as always was present but did not take part in our conversations.

I learned from Ashot a bunch of information that in my opinion was of questionable quality. For example, I learned that the best kebabs are from pork, not lamb. But the pigs must be semi-wild to produce a proper quality meet. This is why in their region they let pigs graze in the mountains. The only problem is that the Azerbaijani steal the Armenians' pigs. On my remark that the Azerbaijani are Muslims and do not eat pork, he replied that I just did not know them. In other conversations Ashot revealed to me that they, the Armenians, are very good soldiers, but need a Russian or some other general to lead them because when the general is Armenian, everyone starts arguing and the battle is lost. I told him that I could relate because we Jews cannot agree on anything and argue with each other also, but that looking at the Israeli army, we managed to overcome at least this challenge.

Another day he told me that there was an Armenian legend that Armenians and Jews are half-brothers. I had never heard anything like this before and asked him to continue. So, according to this legend, a long, long time ago, somewhere in the antiquity, the Armenians were fighting some invaders and lost the battle (a lack of Russian general, I thought to myself). All the men died in that battle, but women and the elderly managed to escape into the mountains. After some time passed, the survivors started realizing that without men their kin would disappear. So, the women collected all their gold and jewelry and bought some Jewish male slaves to continue the stock (I guess the legend meant that the Jewish slaves were bought from Babel, which was on the other slope of the mountains; I doubt they went to Egypt, which was too far and too long ago). After their sons grew up, the Armenians were able to return to their old settlements, and this is what makes Jews and Armenians half-brothers. The legend was nice, except for us being slaves again, but I have never heard it from any other source. All I can say is that the destinies of our two nations is very much alike—genocides and diasporas—so, who knows?

One evening I asked Ashot where he was working in Nagorno-Karabakh, and what he did for a living. He told me that he was the Second Secretary of the local Communist Party Committee.

"Ashot," I said, "don't pull my legs. The secretaries of the party committees are not drafted into this kind of trainings."

"I volunteered," was his response, "We have a big war coming up very soon and I need to learn from Russians how to fight this war."

After that statement I lost the last crumb of trust for this guy and took all our future conversations as pure entertainment. Imagine how surprised I was when in the spring of 1988, just a few months later, I saw the news on TV and in every newspaper about the war suddenly starting in the Nagorno-Karabakh region where the Armenian enclave split from Azerbaijan and declared independence! Ashot was probably one of the leaders of that uprising, and I'd imagine in the ranks much higher than captain. Sorry, Ashot, for not believing you. I may still have some reservations about the stolen pigs, but here you told me the naked truth. And thank you for trusting me with your secrets.

The afterthoughts can actually explain some other mysteries about this group, for example about the second guy. He clearly was not a "servant," but most likely the bodyguard.

Another interesting episode with the Caucasian group happened during our exercises with explosives. The drill was to safely ignite and blow up a dynamite cartridge equipped with a detonating cap and the Bickford safety fuse. The instructors divided us into small groups of eight to ten men and took us to the training ground, an open area surrounded by an L-shaped, earthen embankment. The trainees, one group at a time, were lining up, facing the open area with the embankment behind us and to the right, having only one way of entering and exiting. Everyone had received a dynamite cartridge and a small box of matches. The instructions were to ignite the fuse, lay the cartridge set on the ground in front of you, report to the instructor and wait for the order. Upon the instructor's command, the group in an orderly manner, with emphasis on the orderly, was supposed to exit the field, move behind the embankment, and lie down and count the blasts, making sure that all the cartridges had exploded.

By a mere accident the Azerbaijani guy, Ashot, and I ended up in the same group. When we assumed our positions in the line-up, the Azerbaijani was the furthest to the right, next to the right embankment. To the left of him was Ashot, next to Ashot was me, and then the rest of the group. Upon receiving the command, all of us ignited our cords, lay the cartridges down in front of us and reported ready. All, except the Azerbaijani dude. The trick is that you cannot start the Bickford fuse, we called it a cord, with an open flame. It will melt but not ignite. The technique is to press the match against the powder in a certain way with one hand and strike the match with the box by another hand, opposite to how we usually strike the matches. As I have mentioned earlier, the Azerbaijani did not seem to have any prior training, I have no idea how he graduated his college and got his rank. This time was no exception; he obviously did not have a clue. The fuses were about one meter long, just enough to do the exercise. Here we were, standing in front of our hissing cords and he was monkeying around with his box of matches. Ashot turned to me:

"Can you go and help this idiot?"

"Why me? You are standing next to him."

"No, I cannot talk to him."

Ashot did not move and with an accentuated oriental pride continued staring at his hissing cord.

The salvation came from the rapidly approaching instructor, who probably overheard our conversation because he immediately applied to me with an order to help our troubled comrade. Within a split second the Azerbaijani fuse was hissing in my hands and we, including the instructor, orderly ran to the exit instead of the intended orderly walking, barely making it behind the embankment before the first cartridge blasted off. The last blast was significantly delayed.

A note. I must mention here that the Azerbaijani dude I met at that school in no way represents all the Azerbaijani people. Azerbaijani, as any other people, have well-educated, smart, and intelligent men and women I would probably be humbled to talk to. Plus, I did not even know this man or his story, having never really talked to him. I am just writing about what I have been an eyewitness to, and he happened to be there at that place, at that time, and under those circumstances.

Sundays, our days off, were undoubtedly the best days. We were allowed to leave the campus and go into the city. Remember that the Kaliningrad Oblast was a special military region of Russia with the food supply distinctly different from the other parts of the country. There, for example, you could buy a cup of espresso, which was possible in Kiev, but not in Russia, at least not in places I have lived. Also, in a Kaliningrad cafe you could buy an open sandwich with salami or smoked salmon, which was unheard of even in Kiev. Those sandwiches were our primary food on Sundays for breakfast, lunch, and dinner. My three friends from Kiev and I were always hanging out together. First of course we were having our coffees and sandwiches, then we usually went to the central post office and called home. After that we were free to go anywhere at our fancy, sometimes to the movies, sometimes to the beachfront of the Baltic Sea, sometimes just hanging around.

Once we decided to go to the local Kaliningrad Zoo, and this is the where the next "milestone" event in my life happened. We were standing in front of the lion cage, four of us and some other people, most of them adults with children. The crowd was not big (I am just trying to emphasize that I was not alone). The lion was pacing the cage and suddenly stopped and looked at me, straight in my eyes. There was no threat or anger in his look, just the feeling that he recognized me, the feeling that he had been waiting for me for a long time and finally noticed me and recognized me. That was chilling. Then the lion turned around and sprayed on us, like cats do. We stood far enough away and intuitively jumped aback, so most of the spray fell on the ground, but a few drops marked the bottom of my trench coat.

"Did you see his look?" I asked my friends.

"What look? What are you talking about? Are you OK?"

They looked at me like I was insane. Apparently, I was right, the lion's look and the lion's mark were intended for me, and for me only.

I started frantically thinking of what this may mean—these things do not just happen, it should mean something. Well, I knew that according the horoscope I was born under the constellation of a Lion, this is one. The lion is also the symbol of the tribe of Judah, this is two. Bingo! This is a sign! We are gonna get out of here soon!

Blessed are the believers, regardless of what they believe in, as long as those beliefs do not hurt anyone and give them strength to cope with their circumstances. In my case, the lion's mark was like psychological snap. I had noticed that I became more energetic, more determined, and more confident. I had a feeling that I was being helped. Not by the lion, of course, but by some force that sent me the messenger. The most surprising fact is that after that episode, things with the emigration suddenly started moving, and moving rapidly.

A note. Many years later, living in the United States in the age of internet, I checked my date of birth in the Hebrew calendar. In the year I was born it fell on Elul, not on Av as I was originally thinking and, therefore, my constellation is Virgo, not Leo. This fact leaves me connected to the Kaliningrad lion only through the Judah tribe.

The next Sunday after my encounter with the lion, when I called home, Tatyana told me that she talked to my sister in California and that it looked like the guest visits to the United States are now allowed for close relatives and, if I wanted, my sister could send me an invitation. How would you, my reader, feel about the lion's mark after almost ten years of waiting?

I have two more episodes related to this chapter before we can move on. One evening we were sitting in our barracks watching TV. The news was showing some American man, probably a veteran, who every morning raised the American flag on the flagstaff in front of his house. The Great-Russian nationalistic feelings were in an embryonic stage back then, but were present, in some minds, I knew this from my years in Tula. One of the Russian guys said:

"See how he does it. Why are not we doing the same? Why can they be the patriots of their country and we can't be of ours?"

If I am not mistaken, the guy was from Karaganda, the city in northern Kazakhstan where Russians were a minority. This may explain his brewing nationalistic feelings.

"I can tell you why," I replied. "This American guy raises his flag because he has a house to raise his flag in front of. We do not have anything, where do you want to raise your flag? In the food lines?"

Usually I was restraining myself from opening my mouth under those circumstances because, though most of the guys agreed with me, there was always a good chance of having an informant in such a group. Obviously, the lion's mark loosened my tongue.

Another episode happened toward the end of our term. My homie Vlad needed to make an urgent home phone call on a weekday. He got permission from the curating officer to go after classes and come back before nighttime, but was told to not go alone, to take someone with him. I volunteered, never missing an opportunity to call home. So, we made our calls, had our coffee with sandwiches and were heading back to campus when we were stopped by the military patrol. Our uniform of course gave us away—this is why our colonel insisted that Vlad did not go alone. A lone "partisan" will look too much like unauthorized leave. We showed our military cards and explained the situation. Our military cards were issued in Kiev, so after looking at them, the patrol officer returned them to us with this retort:

"Are you from Kiev?"

We confirmed. And then all of a sudden, he said:

"It should be nice and clean there now, since all the Jews left after the Chernobyl."

I probably looked Slavic enough to him in my uniform. Not recognizing myself I suddenly replied:

"Don't know what you are talking about, comrade captain, I am Jewish, and I live with my family in Kiev."

Fortunately for us, the guy got confused, muttered sorry, and let us go. It could have been much worse if we'd encountered a real asshole. It was interesting to observe the expression on the face of my Ukrainian companion: First surprise, then solidarity and even pride, and then respect.

Lion or not, but those two episodes show how our mentality starts changing when we start smelling a scent of freedom.

A Scent of Freedom

When I returned home, I found two major changes in the status of emigration. The first change was that the Melikha allowed the old "refuseniks," people who were denied in 1979, to re-apply. Don't get me wrong, there was no official announcement or advertisement in the newspaper, we just knew it from some friends who knew other friends. That was a huge step in a positive direction. I expected that in about a year the rest of us would be allowed to go. The second change was that guest visits, which I mentioned before, were now allowed.

It did not make any sense for us to go to the United States as guests, we did not need any additional convictions, we had waited for our chance to leave for years, we knew perfectly what to expect. It made more sense for us just wait a little more and go there for good. That was our initial inclination.

A note. Actually, my image of America from afar was not entirely correct. The Soviet propaganda played a funny joke on me. In essence, my whole image of

America was formed by Soviet propaganda. Not believing anything they say, I turned all their information to the opposite, rotating it 180°. As a result my image was too idealistic, too rosy. I was not, however, disappointed when I saw the reality, I just admitted that the reality never matches the imagination. To the contrary, as an engineer I was very impressed with the American style. I can describe it in two words: Simple and Practical. For example, the Americans would not decorate their subway stations with the stucco molding like the king's palaces because it is not practical. And they would not cover their churches with the gold sheets when half of the population is starving because it is hypocritical. That kind of practicality and simplicity.

Waiting a year or two, however, would not resolve our biggest problem of what to do with Tatyana's parents. We could not take them with us. First, they would not go. Secondly, they were not Jewish, and we knew that in our future endeavors we would have to rely on the support from the Jewish community. Leaving them alone for both of us was morally challenging. At that time, they were in their early sixties and did not need any help from us, but remember, we were leaving forever. On the other hand, we had two children to raise. Things around us were getting worse and worse—overwhelming corruption, society dividing deeper and deeper onto haves and have-nots. Unfortunately, we were among the "have-nots" and had ZERO chance of switching to the other side. Both of us perfectly realized that we would not be able to give our children even as much as we got from our parents, therefore staying there was even more morally challenging. But the scariest part was the nationalistic movements emerging both in Russia and in Ukraine in the wake of the collapsing Empire. The Russian "Pamyat" movement (translated as "Memory") was openly fascistic with armed assault groups attacking liberal intelligentsia. The Ukrainian nationalist movement was still in the embryonic phase, being suppressed by Moscow, but we could see their gatherings on Khreshchatyk Street in downtown. In their speeches and flyers, they were promising to protect us Jews, but who would trust them after centuries of pogroms? And protect from who? From themselves? This was one of the toughest periods in our lives. In addition to all our moral challenges, we were facing a very practical challenge of convincing Tatyana's parents to sign the consent papers. The rule was that the living parents of a person leaving the country for a "permanent settling in Israel" were required to provide a special signed form of consent. We were not sure if her parents would sign their consent. They were simple people living deep in Russia, never exposed to and never interested in anything related to the subject of emigration. According to Soviet propaganda, supported by the TV images, people were dying on the streets of American cities from hunger and cold. Of course, they knew that my sister left, we showed them the letters, and the photos, and the children's clothing my sister was sending us, but in their minds, poisoned by the years of garbage, the letters could have been written in the imperialist torture chambers and the photos could have been fabricated.

Thinking and analyzing all these challenges we started leaning toward the guest visit before we could leave for good. Our logic was simple. If Tatyana and I went there and came back in one piece healthy and happy, her parents would be convinced that it is OK and safe for us to take the kids and move there. Another advantage of going to the United States together was that if their own daughter tells them what she saw there with her own eyes, it may be much more convincing than hearing it from anyone else, including the TV.

No sooner said than done. I called my sister, explained our situation and asked if she and her husband could send the invitation for both of us for couple of weeks. They did not mind. She also wanted to invite my father, but wanted him to stay longer, so we decided that Dad would go there earlier and fly back with us. Tatyana's parents didn't mind taking the kids for a few weeks, either, so the ball started rolling. As soon as we received an invitation, we took it to OVIR (Department of Visas and Registrations) and filled out our applications. Guest visits, when allowed, were easy, we received our permissions within a month or so.

The next challenge was money. This subject requires a little more explanation. My sister and her husband were very generous to buy tickets for both of us, otherwise this trip would not have been possible, we never would have saved enough money to pay for those tickets. But the trip required more money than just the tickets. Those who were leaving the country for a guest visit were allowed to exchange a whopping 300 rubles per person, so both of us could exchange 600 rubles. To our advantage, the Melikha decided to make a show out of these guest visits and was exchanging one ruble for 1.6 dollars, though the real value of the ruble was probably around 10 cents. By comparing the prices of various goods on the black market this became very obvious. For example, the black-market price for a VCR (video cassette recorder) that could be bought in the U.S. for approximately 200 dollars was around 2,000 rubles, hence 1:10. It would be stupid to miss such an opportunity and exchange less than the allowed maximum.

As I have mentioned, there were some people in the Soviet Union who had plenty of money in rubles, but had problems with buying anything using those rubles—in the street slang the rubles were called the "wooden money." One of our friends found such a person for us. This lady, under our friend's guarantee, gave us 1,000 rubles with the condition that we would bring her a VCR. She was taking a risk for a 100% profit, and we got the money we needed: a fair deal.

Now, after getting our permission from Soviet authorities, we had to go to Moscow to get the U.S. visas and retrieve our tickets. That was a pleasant trip, a little peek into another world. My sister bought our tickets through PanAm, which had just started offering their joint Aeroflot/PanAm flights between Moscow and New York. The traveler could buy the tickets through either office, depending on what currency the traveler was using, but all were flying in the same Boeing plane. The fact that our tickets were bought through PanAm helped us a great deal later in New York. When my sister let us know that she received a confirmation that our tickets were waiting for us at the PanAm office in Moscow, Tatyana and I flew to Tula, dropped our kids off with her parents and took a train to Moscow. Although the distance was only 200 kilometers, it took this train more than five hours to get there. Despite that, taking this train early enough in the morning, it was possible to do the whole business in a one-day trip.

Our first destination was the PanAm office to get our tickets. The office was located in the new, modern, limited-access Trade Center in the center of the city. It had sliding doors and quiet, high-speed elevators, which we had never seen before in our lives, despite the fact that we did not come from some god-forsaken province, we came from the second-largest city in the country. The clerk ladies spoke Russian but were unfamiliarly polite. Wow, and we had not even left the country yet!

Our second destination was the American embassy where we just showed up without any appointment because there was no way to make such an appointment. The Marines standing at the entrance like statues were impressive. Many years later I met one electrical foreman, a former Marine, who was deployed to serve at the U.S. embassy in Moscow at about that time. He could have been one of those guys. We showed the clerk our invitations and permissions and, after waiting for about half an hour, were invited for a brief interview. When the gentleman talking to us found out that we were husband and wife traveling together, he became a little uneasy. But when we told him and showed corresponding documents that our two kids were staying home with the grandma, he softened up and stamped our passports. I guess at the beginning he was afraid that we were not planning to come back.

We even had some time left that day to buy some nice presents for our American hosts in the Gorky Street stores, as we now had some money.

Our trip to America took place in the last week of August and the first two weeks of September of 1988. By that time most of the Refuseniks had already left and the departure of the first brave others started. I felt that I should have been among them, but at this point there was nothing we could do but follow our plan.

The flight was from Sheremetyevo Airport in Moscow. We took the same route through Tula and dropped the kids with Tatyana's parents. Back then I was still smoking and in the rush of preparations did not buy my cigarettes in Kiev. In Tula it was hard to find the cigarettes with filters that I used to smoke, and I had to get myself some cigarettes without filters but with a cardboard holder instead. I am not sure if any of the still-living Americans remember those. The name of the product was "Belomor." I bought one pack just to make it to Moscow with intention to buy a block of normal cigarettes for the trip, I did not want to spend my dollars on cigarettes. When we came to Sheremetyevo, I did not find any kiosks, then we rushed through customs, and then the duty-free cigarettes were scarily overpriced, and this is how I unintentionally ended up with the pack of Belomors in America.

At the airport waiting area we noticed a group of people who obviously did not belong to the surrounding environment of luxury and foreignness. All in dark gray clothes, women with headdresses, men in high boots and quilted wadding jackets with the weather-beaten faces of people farming the land. Those were Russian Germans from northern Kazakhstan whose grandparents were interned there during WWII from the Volga region and never allowed to return to their original settlements. West Germany was already quietly taking their own.

The Boeing airplane was very impressive by its size, by comfort of the seats, and of course by the service. The crew was mostly English-speaking, I believe there were a couple girls on the plane who spoke Russian, but I was trying to test my English. This was first opportunity in my life-time to talk to an English-speaking person. The food was excellent, at least by our standards, the portions were big. We did not finish everything they gave us and Tatyana, despite my objections, hid a couple leftover muffins in her purse, which became very useful for us later on. Up this day this is one of her most convincing arguments to prove that she is always right.

The only discomfort for me was that I desperately wanted to smoke. Smoking in the airplanes was already mostly restricted at that time. Only a few rows at the back of the plane were allowed to smoke. On my way to the restroom after dinner, I noticed that a few passengers from the front were standing and smoking in the aisles next to those smoking seats at the back and the flight attendants were not objecting. So, I quickly got back to my seat, pulled my Belomor cigarette with the cardboard holder, walked to the back and joyfully lit it up. The eyes of the flight attendant girl, who just happened to walk by, became large and almost square when

161

she saw me. "No, no," she yelled, "you cannot smoke THIS here" with a strong emphasis on THIS. She made me extinguish my cigarette and told me that I should not even try it again. I realized that it was my cigarette that for some reason made her so excited but could not figure out why. When in San Francisco I told this story to my brother-in-law he started laughing and explained that those cigarettes look a lot like the marijuana joints and the poor girl thought that I was smoking marijuana on the plane. This is how we "Russians" are getting our bad reputation. Have to hand it to her though, she did not even call security, just told me not to do it again.

Our flight was delayed in Moscow for a couple hours and did not make it to New York on time. Our flight to San Francisco left without us. We, and a bunch of other passengers from our plane, were directed to the PanAm service desk for further instructions. So far, I could follow the events, because the announcements on the plane were made in both languages. In JFK we managed to find the PanAm service desk fairly easily by following the signs, but mostly the crowd of late passengers from our flight. This is where the fun began. Talking to the clerk I very quickly realized that she completely understood my questions in English, but I could barely understand her answers in English. It was much tougher than talking to the flight attendant about food or cigarettes. She was talking to me in complete sentences and I could catch only one or two words out of those sentences, if I was lucky. The problem was with the speed, which was too fast for me, and the roaring American pronunciation. The only instructions I carried out from my conversation with the clerk were that we must sit down and wait, confirmed by observing the other fellow passengers doing just that.

A must note here that I studied English for five years at school and for three years in college with good grades. For some reason I liked this subject. Special thanks to my school teacher Zinaida Vladimirovna, a tough and very demanding lady, who did a wonderful job for all her students, half of whom were Jewish and now live in the United States. We've even had class reunions, once in Boston and once in Chicago, where we raised special toasts to her. Ironically, her approach for teaching us English, and she openly declared it to us, was based on assumption that none of us would ever speak to anyone in this language because of the "Iron Curtain." Therefore, she did not care too much about our pronunciation, she probably could not pronounce it correctly herself. But she told us that if any of us were to become a scientist, or a doctor, or an engineer, we would have to be able to translate foreign articles and technical literature, so her emphasis was on that. To accomplish that goal, she made us go far beyond the school program. To get a decent grade from her, we had to go to downtown Kiev and buy the only English-written newspaper allowed in USSR, The Morning Star, issued by the Communist Party of Great Britain. She was giving us certain articles to translate and then discuss in class. I still remember sitting Sundays with a huge dictionary and trying to understand the b.s. written in those articles instead of playing soccer with my buddies outside (probably the best time investment I ever made in my life). After college I was trying to preserve at least that little English that I learned by reading a few adapted fiction books that I could find there. So, at the time of our travel, I could read and more or less understand written texts, but my conversational English was a mess. Tatyana, who was not a huge fan of English classes at school, gave up very soon and was completely relying on my expertise.

Sitting in the waiting area, we met another young couple and, after exchanging a few words (and a cigarette), found that the guy was originally from Yugoslavia, living in the United States for quite a few years. All conversation was in English, but I miraculously understood almost everything this guy was saying because the sound of his words was coming from his lips, like we are used to, not guttural like Americans speak. When the girl at the service desk announced something over the speaker, I did not understand a word again. I had no other choice than to ask my new friend to repeat, and again, understood practically everything. I probably annoyed the hell out of this guy, but he was my only link to the outside world.

An interesting detail was that after a while, another Russian couple, heading to San Francisco, came to the front desk, but they were turned away because they bought their tickets through Aeroflot and PanAm refused to deal with them. We talked to them the next day. They had to spend a night at the airport, kind of like that character in the movie played by Tom Hanks.

Finally, after waiting for a few hours, we were loaded on the buses and taken to a hotel. It was a nice hotel, the Doral on Park Avenue in Midtown—many years later we found it when we were in New York, but it was closed. After waiting for a little longer in the lobby, we received the keys and got to our room. It was already very late at night, we were extremely tired, super hungry, and cold from the air conditioner blowing at full blast. First, I gathered all my engineering skills together and turned that devilish machine from cooling to heat, then we ate the PanAm muffins from Tatyana's purse with a glass of tap water for dinner and went to sleep.

The next morning, we woke up completely refreshed and very hungry. I looked out the window and was amazed with the roof garden just below us. I had never seen such a thing before, the idea of planting a park on the top of a roof was unimaginable, but very practical. Then after a quick shower we went downstairs to the restaurant and had our breakfast. I had a little challenge with the menu because all those words were out of my vocabulary—I had never run across them before, neither in The Morning Star newspaper, nor in the fiction books I was reading, but the waiters were very patient and finally, after asking us if scrambled eggs will do, brought us a beautiful breakfast with eggs, and potatoes, and toasts, and coffee, and even strawberries on a side. We paid $20 for our breakfast, which was a fortune in our circumstances, but did not regret a penny, especially since it included a pack of Marlboros.

We had a couple hours to spare before going back to the airport and decided to explore the area. Logically we understood that we should be somewhere in the city center and that the famous Broadway should be somewhere nearby but were completely disoriented. So, we just decided to walk in a random direction and see what we would find there. It was a cold Sunday morning, the streets were practically empty, some strange people were occasionally passing by, steam was rising up from the street utility lids under our feet, and an odd new feeling suddenly hit me: We were alone on these strange unfamiliar streets of this completely unknown to us far-away city, we are dressed in our Soviet-made dark grayish clothes speaking our foreign-to-anyone-around-us language, and no one in the world cares who we are, where we are, what we think, or what we do.

Is this how the people here, on the other side of the fence, feel themselves? Is this how the free people feel? Is this that sensation of freedom I have been looking for all my cognitive life? I looked at Tatyana—we both liked it!

We did not find Broadway that morning but found the Hudson River instead. On our way back, we also accidentally found the Central Bus Station, which came in very handy later since the bus from PanAm that was supposed to take all of us to the airport did not show up. Some people were taking taxis, but we walked to the Central Bus Station and were able to pay back the kindness of our Yugoslav friend and his lady by showing them the way.

The rest of our trip went without adventure. We were happy to see my sister and her husband at SFO after nine years of separation. My nephew, who was a baby the last time I held him in Chop, was already a big boy, my niece was a teenager. They spoke very little Russian but combined with my little English it was fairly easy to communicate. Generally, the whole trip I was trying to talk and understand as much English as I could and engaging in conversations with everyone I came across. My sister took a couple days off and showed us San Francisco. On this trip she took us to a special store on Polk Street that was selling VCRs and other electronics suitable for European systems. This is where we spent most of our money.

One day we called my school friends from Kiev, a couple smart enough to emigrate the same time as my sister, while they were in their early twenties, pregnant with their first child. A couple months before our trip I met an older sister of one of them in our block's grocery store in Kiev and, when I told her that we were going to visit San Francisco, she gave me their phone number. The guys went a long way in those nine years and were already well-established. My friend picked us up in his Porsche and first took us to their apartment in San Francisco to show us where they lived and then they took us out to dinner at a very nice restaurant, telling their story along the way. Of course, they asked us if we were planning to emigrate and received our definite "yes." The advice we got from our friends that day we later cherished through the toughest years of our immigrant adaptation: Do not look around, it will make you miserable, always go your own way.

The vacation went by fast and it came time to go home. We traveled back together with my dad, again by PanAm with the transfer in New York. Now, being experienced international travelers, we were ready for any challenges, but nothing happened. All planes were on time, we boarded our plane in New York and flew eastward. In the plane my dad approved our decision to go but told us that he would be staying with his wife in Russia. He did not feel comfortable with the language and the whole setup, hinting that this was for young people and he would manage somehow in the place he was then. I was not worried about him too much, because first, I realized that we would be able to help them from outside much more than having him and his wife go with us through the whole immigration process, along with our two kids. Secondly, that between my sister and I we would be able to take them in later on when we settled.

The reality of returning hit me when I was still in the airplane pre-composing my conversation with customs in English and suddenly realizing that I did not need English any more, that those for whom I was preparing my speech spoke Russian. We were returning to Egypt, to our jail, a big jail, one-sixth of the Earth's dry land, but jail, nonetheless.

Overall the trip was a complete success. We brought our creditor a requested VCR, sold everything else at a good market price and convinced Tatyana's parents that contrary to what they had seen on TV, life in America is much better than in the U.S.S.R. as long as a person is able and willing to work. Our psychological calculations proved to be right and worked as planned. Tatyana's mother, being grandma Lisa's daughter, was always a very practical person. A simple fact that we went there without any money and came back with money spoke to her much louder than any TV.

The Exodus

The Jewish emigration from the Soviet Union up to 1990 was almost exclusively to "Israel, the country conditional." This is what was written in our exit visas. It did not necessarily mean that everyone moved to Israel, but it meant that almost everyone exited the country of origin using Israeli visas. The reason for the exit was shown as "family re-unification," the purpose as "permanent settlement." After the 1967 war, the Soviet Union and Israel did not have diplomatic relations, therefore the exit was through a third country, i.e., Austria. The absence of diplomatic relations had several other consequences. One of them was that the Soviet authorities could not verify through proper diplomatic channels if an applicant had any relatives in Israel and how close those relatives were. Therefore, any Jew could claim relatives in Israel and ask for permission to go. The only document we needed to show was an invitation from those relatives, certified by the Israeli authorities. Since we are all members of the same tribe and, I'd guess, out of contempt for the

Kremlin for what they did to us and to the State of Israel, the Israeli authorities did not mind stamping any invitation from anyone to anyone. I am not sure what Jewish organization took care of those invitations, but if any Jewish person anywhere in the free world would come to a local Jewish community center and give the names and the addresses of his or her friends or relatives in the Soviet Union who wanted to emigrate, an invitation would be sent.

This is exactly what my sister did, giving our names and address to someone in the Jewish Community Center in Oakland, California. Now we had to wait. This was the longest and the most difficult waiting period I ever experienced in my life both before and after. Waiting for the end of military service or waiting for retirement, which is what I am doing now, is a leisurely walk with a kindergartener, compared to that wait. I went completely insane checking our mailbox several times a day and chasing Gypsy fortune-teller women at every bus and railroad station, during my continuing business trips, with request to tell me my fortune. My friends, traveling with me, started getting really worried about my mental state and were trying to keep me away from those fortune-tellers because usually it's supposed to be other way around, with the fortune-tellers annoying the potential clients.

A note. By the way, none of the Gypsy fortune-tellers gave me any, even the slightest, hints of what was ahead of me. Maybe it is true that the fortune of a Jewish person is not predictable and is entirely in the hands of the Highest Authority. Or maybe the Gypsy fortune-tellers I met in Ukraine were not the good ones and were just collecting easy money off the shlemazels and schlemiels like me.

It took us four long months to finally find that cherished elongated envelope with Hebrew letters on the post stamp in our mailbox. Remembering how abruptly it ended ten years ago, I was afraid to lose a minute and the next morning went straight to OVIR. To register the invitation and fill out the initial paperwork I had to go to our local Pechersky district OVIR department, which was just a small room in the local police office. After that, all the following documentation, interviews, permits and everything else were processed through the central city OVIR office. During my sister's wave of emigration, the city OVIR office was in the center of Kiev, on Shevchenko Boulevard. The huge lines at the entrance and crowds of excited Jews on the surrounding streets looked very provocative and probably annoyed the ruling authorities. This is why, I am guessing, when we were leaving, they moved the OVIR office to the unnoticeable industrial and warehouse area called Saperka, fortunately for us within walking distance from where we lived. Again, how did we know where to go and what to do is a mystery to me now, the grassroots network must have been working at full bandwidth.

For the first visit to the local police office I went alone, and Tatyana stayed home with the kids. The line was not long, with only one guy who looked Arabic in front of me. We started talking, he turned out to be a student from Syria. When he asked me where I was going, (remember, it was the visa office) and I replied Israel, I expected an if not violent but at least negative reaction. To my surprise the reaction was rather positive and kind of sad:

"You guys are lucky to have a place to go."

"What are you talking about? Syria is a relatively free country, you can go pretty much anywhere you want."

"You are helping each other, we don't."

I did not understand him back then, I understand him now.

In the office I presented my invitation to the clerk and told her that our family wanted to go to Israel for a permanent settlement. Her question, "Why?" took me by surprise. Was it not obvious why? After so many years of waiting and living in the parallel reality, my mind froze. It took me a few seconds to concentrate:

"I want to reunite with my family in Israel."

"How are you related to the person in this invitation?"

"This is a brother of my grandfather."

"Where is your grandfather?"

"He passed away in 1974."

"Are you planning to live in Israel with your relative?"

"Yes, the man is getting old and needs our help."

"Will any of your close relatives remain in Soviet Union?"

"Yes, my father."

"I see, after that your family will become really united . . ."

She smiled and took my paperwork. If I remember correctly, she gave me our application forms with the written instructions, which we had to fill out at home, collect and attach a bunch of other documents, and send everything to OVIR by mail. This included the consent from our parents that I mentioned earlier. It probably took us another month or so to get this done.

A note. Again, it would be naive to think that the KGB, the OVIR, and the rest of them did not know what was going on. We all realized that we were just pawns in the much bigger political game of that time. I am not sure what price President Reagan had to pay Gorby for letting us go, but thank you, Mr. President, whatever it was!

Most likely it was beneficial and convenient for all parties to play the game of family reunification, so we played our parts.

Upon sending our applications, I quit my job at the electrical startup office. It was sad because I worked there with my very good friends whom I knew since high school, but I had to stay in Kiev to be ready at any time. As I mentioned, we had some money left from our trip to America, but we did not know how long the process might take and did not want to risk living on this money. So, I started looking for some temporary job. Help once again came from my Uncle Semion. At that time, he was working as a head of a mechanical department (in American terminology it would be operation and maintenance) in one of the construction offices and did not mind hiring me as an electrician. For me it was a great benefit because I perfectly realized that I would not be working as an engineer in America, at least not for the first few years; therefore, learning the trade would not hurt.

My uncle of course knew my situation very well and did not load me up too much. There I befriended a guy named Alex, who was working as a welder. He was also Jewish, a few years younger than me. He was a pretty good welder and we worked together as a team, he welding the pipes and I pulling wires through them. Over there we could not even imagine that the materials like EMT conduits existed. When we met, Alex was not even thinking about emigration, but when we parted, he was ready to go, all due to my bad influence. His worry was that he was not an engineer, but just a simple welder, so what was he gonna do there? I told him about the American middle class and explained that a good welder in America is in much higher demand than an engineer. I am wondering where he is now.

One morning, about a month into my new career, Uncle Semion called me into his office and asked me if I could fix a starter on a motorized hoist. Working for a few years as an electrical startup engineer, I confidently answered yes. The issue was that on one of the critical construction sites, one of two hoists lifting the materials to the upper floors quit working. The site, already behind schedule, significantly slowed down and they urgently needed someone to come and fix it.

I took my screwdriver and pliers, jumped on the city bus and went across town to a site in Darnitsa on the left bank. The whole job took me a few minutes. It was something very simple, if I am not mistaken, the Start and Stop push buttons were wired incorrectly or something like that. I remember being surprised that this thing ever worked before. The construction manager was very happy, but when I asked if I could go told me no and gave me an assignment to stay right there next to the hoist for the rest of the day and make sure that nothing happened to it. All my assurances that it would work fine now went in vain. But that was not the end of the story. The next morning, Uncle Semion called me again to his office and informed that he received a call from upper management, and that they were very happy with my performance and requested me to be on that site next to the hoist until the end of construction or for as long as the hoist is there. This is how I spent a good third of my electrician career in Kiev watching the perfectly working hoist. My curse of fixing the printer followed me from Kaliningrad.

At the same time, we were getting ready for our departure, to use the slang of those times, "Otval" (which can be translated either as "debarking" or as "falling away"). Firstly, my father came to Kiev and claimed permanent residence to preserve the apartment flat. Secondly, we were trying to buy some optics and other goodies that could be sold in Italy, which I had described earlier. It was not an easy task. In addition to being always in short supply, those items became in high demand with the growing emigration. On this front we received help from Tatyana's cousin Vitaly in Leningrad who fully supported our decision. Vitaly had very good connections and could buy practically anything. Thanks to G-d and our trip to America, we now had some money. We were carefully planning what we could carry with us on our long journey. Having four hands and assuming that the kids would not be running away, we obviously could not plan to carry more than four items. Those items would preferably be on wheels because the items for sale in Italy were heavy. The wheeled suitcases, so common in the West, just started appearing in the Soviet Union stores. It took us a lot of effort to find them. We still have one of those suitcases in our attic as memorabilia. Everything else, all our possessions that we could not carry with us, we were either trying to sell or were giving away to our friends.

And, of course, we were regularly visiting OVIR, mostly me. You'd go to that place of disappointments and hopes in the morning and take your place in line. Then, by about noon you'd get to the clerk's desk and ask if there were any updates on your case. The clerk would tell you none, come back in couple weeks. You'd come back in couple weeks and repeat the drill. The only positive outcome from those visits was that you'd stay in line for hours with people who were in the same boat as us. This is where the major exchange of anecdotes, rumors, and very valuable information took place.

I remember one episode that happened in the spring, around Passover time. I was standing in line with the rest of the crowd when suddenly a man with the matzah sticking out of his netted bag showed up in our line. Everyone got excited and started asking him where he found the product because matzah was never sold in any stores, it was one of the prohibited items. For that reason, carrying the matzah openly in the netted bag looked defiant enough to get everyone's attention.

"Guys, you will not believe it. On my way here, I was walking along Proreznaya (a well-known street in the center of Kiev) and bam! There is a kiosk selling matzah right there on that street! I could not just walk by, I had to buy some!"

Everyone stared in confusion for a second and then a voice out of the crowd ironically asked:

"Hey guys, maybe we should stay now?"

And immediate answer from that crowd:

"Thank you, but too late!"

Everyone started laughing. This episode is an example of the atmosphere we were living in. The common joke of those times was that the Jews could be divided in three categories: those who already left, those who are going to leave, and those who think that they are not going to leave, but will leave anyway.

My biggest worry was to be too late and to get stuck there for another ten years. Regarding the destination, we did not worry that much about where we were going, we just wanted to get out.

A note. The events I am describing in this chapter happened in the spring and summer of 1989, the Soviet empire collapsed only two short years later in December of 1991. In 1989 we did not know that the empire was collapsing, none of us could predict this happening. So, it would be wrong to say that we left because the empire was collapsing. We left because we could not and did not want to live like that anymore. Can someone conjecture that the empire collapsed because we left? Objectively, probably not. From the religious-historical point of view, maybe, who knows?

Our approval finally came in early June of 1989. It took them a little more than four months to process our case. Now we had mounds of work to do and I did not want to lose even one minute.

First, we gave away our passports in exchange for pieces of paper with our names typed (literally typed with a typewriter) in the Russian language. My paper had my photo glued to it, Tatyana's had a photo of her and our twelve-year-old daughter, but no photo of our four-year-old son. Both kids' names were written on Tatyana's piece of paper. The documents were called the "exit visas." For this procedure and those two pieces of paper we paid 760 rubles per adult person. Remember, I was earning 200 rubles a month. This is the reason we needed all that money we made from our trip to America. We also received a letter informing us that by the special session of the Supreme Soviet we were now stripped of our Soviet citizenship and were not under the protection of the U.S.S.R. any longer.

A note. At that time in the U.S.S.R. there were many cases of Russian women marrying foreign students from African and Arab countries. When those women were leaving the U.S.S.R. to settle with their husbands in the countries of their husbands' origin, the Russian women and their children were retaining

Soviet passports and citizenship and could return home any time they wished under the protection of the Soviet government. So, if my Russian wife, for example, married a Syrian Arab and went with him to settle in Syria, she and her children would remain Soviet citizens. But since she had married me, a Soviet Jew, and was going with me to settle a few miles south of Syria in Israel, she and her children were stripped of their Soviet citizenship. If this is not an example of racism and anti-Semitism in its purest form, I do not know what is!

If I am not mistaken, the next step was to go to the local Military Commissariat and turn in my military card. I may be mixing the sequence of events here, it was a long time ago. This is where I learned that I almost made it to the rank of captain. The colonel was very disappointed when he heard the reason for my visit and revealed to me that following my school in Kaliningrad, I was recommended for my next rank and they were just waiting for me to be approved and were about to call me in for the upcoming military exercises. Sorry Comrade Colonel, I am out!

In OVIR they also informed us that we had to upgrade all our birth certificates, marriage certificate, and diplomas with the foreign format documents because the originals would not be allowed to leave the country. That meant a trip to Tula.

In addition, we needed to get the Israeli, Austrian, and Czechoslovakian stamps on our so called "exit visas" to be able to cross the border. Austria and Czechoslovakia had consulates in Kiev, so those visas were easy. Israel did not have diplomatic relations with the Soviet Union—or I should probably say it was vice versa because the Soviet Union was the side that broke the relations in 1967 after losing the war. The Israeli visas could only be obtained in the Netherlands embassy in Moscow, which at that time represented the interests of Israel in the U.S.S.R., and that meant a trip to Moscow.

For us it was already a well-known and familiar route. We flew to Tula, left the kids with grandma, took a train to Moscow, boom-boom all in one day, and back to Tula late at night. This was the last time we saw Moscow, and I am OK with that, no special feelings.

In Tula we expected a negative reaction from the local authorities while exchanging our documents to the foreign format. To our surprise, the reaction was very positive. The woman in City Hall who signed our papers, the People's Deputy, was very friendly and wished us good luck. At my college the reaction was the same, very friendly. By the way, the foreign format documents were practically the same, all written in Russian, they just looked newer. My guess is that the Melikha was just trying to collect more money.

We returned to Kiev with Tatyana's parents because the day of departure was rapidly approaching. My father came to Kiev, too. His situation also changed rapidly. His wife's only daughter, my new stepsister in Rostov, decided to go, too (which was very brave of them because both she and her husband were musicians), which would leave my elderly dad and his wife in the country alone, meaning that they would have to follow us ASAP.

In Kiev we stamped our exit visas in the Austrian and Czechoslovakian consulates and that made us ready to buy the tickets. Our point of destination was Vienna, Austria, the closest democratic country on the map of Europe at that time to the west of us. The options for reaching Vienna were limited to either flying or taking a train. Flying needed to be booked months in advance and we did not want to waste a minute. There was only one direct train between Moscow and Vienna with a short stop in Kiev that we could use, but that train was coming already packed from Moscow with a very limited number of seats available for people getting on in Kiev. Booking, again, could take months. So, we decided to take the most common route, the same route my sister took ten years before us. Take a train to the Chop border-crossing point, then to Bratislava and eventually to Vienna. The tickets we bought were between Kiev and Vienna, meaning that we paid for the whole trip in rubles, but the seats were assigned only to Chop.

Our visas allowed us to exchange our money for U.S. dollars, $90 per person, $360 for our whole family of four. Rubles were not allowed to cross the border; even though they could only be used as toilet paper, no one in the world would ever exchange rubles for any currency. Whatever the life savings the emigrant families had, had to be left behind. For our family it was super easy. All we had was leftovers from our trip to America, which we were gladly leaving to our parents. Our life savings were our two kids, my college degree, and our thirst for freedom which they could not take away from us. Possession of U.S. dollars in the Soviet Union was a crime punished by jail, so at the exchange place we had received accompanying paper confirming that we had temporary permission to possess this amount of dollars and authorizing us to take these dollars across the border. I hid both the dollars and the permission separately deep in the most unreachable places in our twenty-five-square-meter flat, too deep as it turned out later.

Our train to Chop was departing on June 26th, 1989, this date we remember. It took us three weeks from the date of permission to the date of departure, and I'd say we did a pretty good job. The last ritual was a traditional farewell party, the event of significance primarily to those who were staying behind rather than to those who were leaving, and this is why: Keep in mind that we were still living in the Soviet Union, our apartment was most likely under KGB surveillance, and coming over to the farewell party required some guts, especially for our non-Jewish friends. Some of them came to the party, others came to the railroad station and stood with us, "the betrayers of the motherland," publicly on the platform. Kudos to all of them, this could have been their first show of defiance to the system, their first step in the search of their own freedom.

When the day came, we took a taxi to the railroad station, fortunately way before our departure time, planning to have enough time to say our last farewells to all our friends and family. Our train was supposed to go through Korosten, my father's hometown, where he had not been for quite a while and where some of his cousins were still living. So, he bought himself a ticket on the same train with the intention to get off in Korosten. We also had Dimitry, my sister's brother-in-law, the same guy who was with me accompanying my sister to Chop ten years earlier. Dimitry volunteered to go again, this time with us.

A note. Dimitry and his family came to California a couple years later.

So, there we were, standing on the platform, waiting for our train, chatting with our small seeing-off group, when one of my friends suggested I check one last time that all of the paperwork was with us. I laughed that it was not much paperwork to check—here are our visas, here are the tickets, here are the dollars, here is . . .? The permission to take the dollars across the border was left behind at home! At first there was disbelief, then panic, then yelling at me (and rightfully so), then questioning what to do. One of my cousin's husband, Fima, came with a car, parked at the station, and volunteered to help. We had roughly an hour before departure. If we were lucky, theoretically we could make it in half an hour each way. The problem was that it was already afternoon and the traffic was starting to build up. But there were no other options, so we decided to go. The plan was, if I was late, Tatyana, the kids, and Dimitry would go as planned and wait for me in Chop. Having traveled for the last four to five years all over Ukraine, I would find my way somehow, maybe the next day.

No sooner said than done. Fima and I ran to the car, stepped on the gas and drove back to our apartment to the amusement of our neighbors who had given me a final farewell just an hour ago. Fima stayed in the car with the engine running, I flew up to our fifth floor (mind you, there was no elevator in the building), found the paper just where I left it, rushed back practically jumping down the whole stairwell sections, dove into the car and we sped back to the station. This leg of the trip we made in decent time, but, as we expected, the traffic already started building up.

With my frequent travels I knew the layout of the Kiev railroad station like the back of my hand with all of its ins and outs. There was a tunnel under the tracks for taking passengers from the station building to the platforms, typical of all railroad stations in the world. But I knew that this tunnel was not dead-ended at the last platform but had an exit to the city street at the opposite side of the tracks. This exit was little-known and was used mostly by locals. If we went there, to the other end of the tunnel, we could bypass the jammed city center streets and the station plaza. So, I asked Fima to change the route and drive to Solomenka, explaining to him my new plan on the way. He did not know about that exit and agreed that it might work. It took us an eternity to get there. Fima dumped me at the mouth of the tunnel and I ran as fast as I could. When I emerged out on my platform the train was still there, I looked at my watch, it was two minutes before the departure time, we made it! So, when I am saying now that I ran out of the Soviet Union, I mean it, literally.

A note. My cousin Lora with her husband Fima, along with my two other cousins and their families now live in Israel. Every time we go there, we remember this episode laughing and cheering with adult beverages. Actually, they told us that this visit to the railroad station for our farewell was the turning point in their decision to emigrate.

Then life played another joke with us. After I jumped onto the train, the train did not move for another couple hours. According to our conductor, we were delayed because of some problems somewhere down the line. There were no inter-train radio announcements as we are used to here in the United States. The train just stood and stood, and nobody knew why, so we could only rely on what the conductor told us. All our seeing-off party had already left, so we took our seats and were just waiting for departure. When the train finally moved, I was a little surprised because it moved in the wrong direction. The city of Chop, the border we were aiming for, the countries of Czechoslovakia and Austria, all of it was to the West of us, but for some reason our train started moving East! As I have mentioned, I knew the layout of this station very well and could not mix up the direction, we were definitely moving East. When we crossed to the east bank of the Dnieper River, I became really worried and went to talk to the conductor again. I realized that the chances of the Melikha sending the whole train to Siberia for the sake of only my family were minuscule, that they could find some other, more efficient and less costly ways to get us, but no one can blame me for all kinds of weird thoughts under those circumstances. The conductor told me again that something happened down the road and instead of taking the usual northern route we were now talking the southern route. I did not calm down until I saw our train crossing the Dnieper River again by other bridge downstream, this time in the right, western direction. This meant that we were not going through Korosten and my dad was now going with us all the way to Chop.

A note. That time was very disturbing in Eastern Europe. The Solidarity movement in Poland, the demonstrations in Hungary and Czechoslovakia, the mass escapes of East Germans to the West Germany side. All these events were constantly disturbing the system, while the empire was already on the brink of falling apart. The Melikha was trying to quench the disturbances by moving a large number of troops into these countries, but it seemed that nobody cared any more, the Melikha was losing its grip. At the Chop border crossing we witnessed a massive movement of troops in a western direction. In fact, this movement interfered and almost stopped our movement westward. So, my guess is that the relocation of troops was the reason why our train was delayed in Kiev and why it had to take the alternative route.

As soon as we arrived in Chop the next morning, while Dimitry and my father were helping Tatyana with the luggage and kids, I ran to the cashier window for our tickets to Vienna.

The cashier told me that the seats and the tickets would be assigned before the Bratislava train departure in the evening, wrote my name on the waiting list, and gave me a number.

The situation in Chop was completely different from ten years ago. First, there were not as many departing emigrant families as back then, no rush with taking off and unloading the luggage. Second, there were no border patrols. I'd guess that nobody changed the rules about the restricted border zone, but the boys had not received their order to intimidate us and did not care enough to do it themselves. In any case, this time nobody bothered either Dimitry or my dad even once. Honestly, I did not even recognize the station. Maybe they did some remodeling, but most likely it was due to my different perspective, this time being the departing one.

So many years later most of the events of that evening are blurry, but some details still stand out like it happened yesterday. I remember that we ate a very good dinner in the cafeteria, the last hot meal for the kids in the upcoming journey. Then porters showed up with the carts we needed for moving through customs and offered them for a ridiculous price which we accepted because we did not have any other choice. Then, closer to evening time, we started finding out about the delays for our train. It was on and off, on and off, late into the night. The kids were tired, everyone was frustrated. There were probably around ten families trying to get out, we were second in line. Then the porters showed up again and whispered to us confidentially that the train was standing on the platform and if we didn't do anything, would leave without us. It was not that the porters were so considerate, they just wanted to collect their money. So, I decided to talk to the station manager, which unexpectedly made me the spokesman for the whole pack. The cashier pointed me in a direction of a man who just happened to be standing and talking to someone in the hall. This is where, while approaching, I accidentally overheard the word "echelon," which in Russian has only one meaning—the troop train. At my "excuse me," the station manager responded with yelling at me in the sense that he did not have time to talk to my kind because he had people to move. That statement made me explode. I started yelling back at him that if we are not "people" enough for him, he better watches out because as soon as I cross this fricken border, I will let everyone know how he treated us, listing off all human rights organizations that I could think of, starting for some reason with Amnesty International. I guess I was not a good spokesman because the negotiations ended right there with him walking away.

After that it became obvious that nothing was going to happen that night and Tatyana took

Boris to the station's second-floor mother's room where there were a couple small beds for kids.

About half an hour after that the porters suddenly showed up again, this time yelling, "Quickly! Quickly!" grabbing and placing our luggage on the carts. Then the cashier's window opened, and I heard the names called to come over and pick up the tickets, including mine. Dimitry and my dad ran upstairs to bring over Tatyana and kids. Everything was happening so fast! The double doors opened, and the customs officer invited the first family in; they quickly disappeared inside. Tatyana was not there yet:

"Who is next?"

"I am."

"Are you traveling alone?"

"No, they are coming!"

"I do not have time to wait, next!"

"Here are our papers!"

"I do not care about your papers! Are you coming or not? Who is next?"

"Here they are!"

At that second, I saw Tatyana with the kids and the whole entourage on the top of the stairs. Dimitry, holding Masha's hand, ran in first. There were already two of us, and the porter pushed our cart in. Tatyana, with Boris in her hands, and some shmatas flying behind her, slipped through the doors! Done, we were in!

The officer pointed to the big table, the porter put the cart next to the table and left. His part was done. All his job consisted of was pushing the cart through the door. The officer commanded us to open our suitcases, I placed them on the table and started opening. Faster! He grabbed one of the suitcases and turned it upside down, emptying everything onto the table. Three other suitcases met the same fate.

"What do you have? You cannot take this, and this, and this!"

The officer was going through our possessions putting aside one item after another. The "cannot" pile was growing and the "can" pile was shrinking in front of our eyes. But at this moment I did not care anymore, I just wanted to get out.

"Are you the one that was going to complain?"

The voice was coming from the other side of the table. I lifted my eyes from the table and saw another officer who might have snuck in. The guy obviously talked like a higher rank.

"What else do you have? Are you hiding something? Do you want to go with me to a special room?'

"I do not have anything, I can go with you anywhere you tell me to go."

"Sure?"

"Sure."

Boris started crying, Masha looked frightened, Tatyana was holding both of them trying to calm them down. I was ready to go with him to any special room they wanted and let them turn my guts inside out just to have it be over with. But the man suddenly turned around and left, telling his subordinate to continue. It appeared that the whole show was staged especially for me for my big mouth.

A few minutes after the boss left, the other guy pushed the whole "cannot" pile towards us, told us to pack everything quickly and left. Tatyana and I looked at each other in disbelief and started stuffing our suitcases indiscriminately in a rush. Masha was helping us, Boris stopped crying and was trying to help, too.

Neither of us clearly remembers if there were armed soldiers on the platform, like in my sister's case. I believe there were, but we were so tired both physically and emotionally that it did not even catch our attention. The time was around 2 a.m.

The Czechoslovakian train between Chop and Bratislava was a regular commuter train, similar to Russian trains but with cushioned seats, which was already progress. The benches were facing each other with a small table in between. Each bench was for three seats. The Soviet authorities allowed only three families to leave that night, us and two other families, so the train departed practically empty. Naturally, they placed our three families in the same car. As soon as we got in, we placed our luggage on the top shelf and laid the kids on the benches to let them catch at least some sleep. Five minutes after departure the Czechoslovakian customs boarded the train. It was a very tall big lady in a dark uniform with some shining regalia and rolled-up sleeves. Sorry, but she looked like a member of the Nazi SS brigades in the movies. With a very loud voice in broken Russian she commanded us to wake up the kids and sit them up because the seats were assigned, and we had only four seats, not six. All our assurances that we would do exactly as she ordered as soon as the first passengers showed up went in vain. So, we sat up our sleeping kids. Then she told us to show her any jewelry or photo equipment in our luggage, informing us that all that is subject to the Czechoslovakian customs duties and gave us custom declarations to fill out. Nowhere in my grapevine sources or in the OVIR lines had I heard that we ought to pay anything to the Czechoslovakian customs, so I said and marked everything as "No." She left without search. As soon as she left, we laid the kids back down on the benches and took a nap ourselves until the first passengers started to show up around 5 a.m.

Our train arrived at Bratislava late that morning, around 10 a.m. Before the arrival some men approached us several times, offering to exchange dollars for koruna, arguing that we would have to eat in Bratislava anyway and that their exchange rate was much better than the official one at the railroad station. We were very cautious about these offers and abstained, plus we still had some food from home. The other two families yielded and exchanged.

Now a little about our fellow travelers. One of the families was a young couple in their mid-twenties with no children. They were both engineers from Perm, a large industrial city in the Ural region of Russia—I did not even know that there were Jews that far east. The guys were very pleasant and easygoing, they hoped to get to New York. Unfortunately, I don't remember their names. The second family was from Kishinev, Moldova. The couple, Semion and Lilia, were a little older than us—their older son was around sixteen vs our Masha, who was only twelve. They were emigrating with their entire family—them, two kids, her parents, and his parents, a total of eight people. Everyone was giving them respect for the bravery. Semion was a taxi driver in Kishinev, what Lilia's occupation was we did not know. Their point of destination was Los Angeles, where they had some relatives. Between the two children and four parents, who were constantly competing for attention, especially in those circumstances, their family was always yelling and screaming, a typical Jewish bazaar. Lilia was always very busy, tense and sad. In a rare quiet moment when she could just sit down with her eyes and corners of her lips down, Semion used to tell her "Honey, spit out the lemon," which made her smile.

We all kept together throughout our Czechoslovakian journey and met a couple times in Vienna.

We arrived in Bratislava. We all knew from our grapevine sources at home that we would have to hire porters in Bratislava and that the price was two bottles of vodka per cart. As soon as we unloaded our luggage on the platform, the porters came to us offering their service. From that point on we all stuck together as a pack. We did not argue, just confirmed the price. As I have mentioned, we had very little luggage, only four suitcases. At the same time Semion's family had a lot of luggage, all of which would not fit on one cart. So, Semion and I made a deal and split one cart between us, giving the porters four bottles for two carts, three bottles from him and one bottle from us. The deal saved us a bottle of vodka. Remember, my reader, that vodka was our currency. The limit through the Soviet customs was two bottles per adult. The procedure for disposing vodka was giving whatever it would take to the porters in Bratislava and then selling the rest in Vienna, no one was even thinking of consuming the product. Where and how we were supposed to sell vodka in Vienna we did not know, all we knew was that vodka should not be brought to Italy, it was not sellable there.

The porters pushed our luggage carts to the other platform and told us that our train would depart from there at 6 p.m., that the luggage was safe now and we could relax. Then they took our vodka and left, leaving our luggage in the middle of the empty platform on the carts. Communication with the porters was easy enough because their language was Slavic. After the porters had left, we had a little safety meeting and decided that we should not trust them and would verify the platform ourselves and take turns watching our stuff.

We had plenty of time and, when our family was relieved from the watching duty, decided to go out of the railroad station and at least glance at the city. As soon as we left the station, right there on the plaza we spotted a hot dog stand, looking exactly like what we had seen in America. I approached the stand, asking in English if they would accept dollars, and heard a definite "Yes!" Then I asked how many hotdogs I would get for one dollar, and after short negotiations we settled on six. With all the condiments and attributes, that was the deal we were looking for! Actually, when we took all our hot dogs to an outside table, we discovered that they gave us seven. Seven hotdogs for one dollar, this is how far his majesty's buck can go!

The kids munched two hot dogs each in a minute, Tatyana and I split the other three. It was worm and very delicious food that kept us running for the rest of the day. Our gut feeling not to exchange dollars for korunas turned out to be right.

That evening our train departed on time and from the platform the porters took us to in the morning. The porters came back when the train arrived and helped us with our luggage. To my surprise, the train was packed. A few seats from us I noticed someone speaking English and started listening. It was an American couple in their fifties, probably traveling. I overheard them asking the conductor who were those people, pointing at us. "Oh, those are Russian refugees," was the answer. This was the first time I heard this title applied to me.

A few minutes after the departure, the train stopped at the border crossing and Austrian customs walked in with a small schnauzer-looking dog. The guys were very friendly, smiling all the time, and did not care about our luggage a bit, except for the dog that was running along the car sniffing around, probably looking for drugs. They checked our paperwork and gave each kid a candy. What a difference! Free people are rarely mean. I exchanged a few words with them in English. The American man probably heard this exchange and, after customs left, came to me and we started talking to the best of my ability. He was very surprised that I could speak English and kept asking me multiple questions about who we are and where we were going. I told him the way it was, that we were Jewish refugees from the Soviet Union, that I had a sister in California, and that we did not know yet where we would end up but hoped it would be the United States.

The trip from Bratislava to Vienna was very short, maybe a couple hours at most. When the train arrived at Vienna, we let everyone leave and then unloaded our stuff onto the platform, helping each other. In a few minutes the crowd from our train dissolved and we ended up standing alone in the middle of the platform. OK, we have arrived, now what?

Our goal was Vienna. We knew that we must make it to Vienna and someone would be there to meet us. How did we know? Who will be meeting us? What organization? Address? Phone number? Nothing! We stood on the platform for about half an hour and decided to move our luggage closer to the station. OK, it kept us busy for a while, then we were standing closer to the station. Time was passing by, no one was meeting us. I was feverishly thinking: Well, I have my sister's number, but how can she help us from California? We have some money, at least we can feed the kids. Should we go to police and tell them who we are? Probably this is the only choice . . . Dusk was falling. Let's wait a little more, a little more, a little more . . . Neither Tatyana nor I can recall now how long the waiting was. For us it was an eternity, in reality probably a couple hours. Someone can say: "What are a couple hours compared to nine years of waiting!" Well, this was a different kind of waiting.

Suddenly they showed up. A man and a woman quickly walked toward us from the railroad station, they recognized us on the spot. In broken Russian with a heavy American accent they were giving us their short orders. Go, go! Quickly, quickly! We grabbed our suitcases and rushed, following them through the station out to the plaza toward a minivan parked at the curb. We quickly loaded the luggage, jumped in, took our seats, and went into the city lights. Masha was sitting next to the window, looking outside. "Like it?" I asked. She nodded and smiled.

A note. These men and women who were collecting us at the railroad stations, bus stations, airports, and who knows where else, were American volunteers. Their operation was very simple, lean, and effective. Their budget was based on charities and very limited, but they have not missed anyone, not one person was lost or left without help, and I am talking about tens of thousands. What they did was on the brink of a miracle, almost like the work of Angels. To them I say: Thank you, guys, from the bottom of our hearts.

The van stopped and to our disappointment only Semion's family was ordered out, thus separating us from our new friends. After about ten or fifteen minutes the van stopped again, this time our family was ordered out along with the couple from Perm. We took our suitcases from the back of the van and received short and clear further instructions:

1. Go through this door and up to the third floor, they will show you the place.

2. Be here at this same spot tomorrow at 6 a.m.

Period. This was it.

We walked to the third floor and were shown our room. The place resembled our communal apartments in Russia—a common hall, a common kitchen, a common restroom with a shower, and several rooms. Our room was big, with four beds. We were hungry. We pulled out two packs of Yugoslavia's dry chicken noodle soup from our luggage and went to the kitchen. While preparing soup, we met our new neighbor Eva, a middle-aged woman traveling alone to Los Angeles where she had a daughter. Those who had children in the U.S. were not sent to Italy and underwent different procedures. Anyway, Eva had been stuck in Vienna for a couple months and knew all the ins and outs, meeting and seeing off families like ours. She distinguished herself from others by speaking Yiddish, which was, at least to my ear, very close to the brand of German language the Austrians were speaking. In any case she freely communicated with the locals, which naturally made her the head of our little commune. When Eva heard that we just arrived and had to be at the door at 6 a.m. the next morning, she explained to us that tomorrow we would go through an interview and it would take the whole day. Finding out that this soup was our last food, she offered us a couple of her sandwiches to feed the kids tomorrow on the condition that we return the favor when we settled. Thank you, Eva!

The soup was the best Yugoslavian dry chicken noodle soup we ever had, and the beds were as soft as clouds.

The next morning at 6 a.m. sharp we were standing outside, armed with Eva's sandwiches and fresh hopes. While waiting, we wrote down our new address, just in case, the number from the building, the street name from the street sign, in our little green oilcloth-covered notebook. In this notebook we kept our vital information, like my sister's address and telephone number, our parents' telephone numbers, and so on. I could have reproduced this Vienna address here because we still have this notebook, but do not want to disturb the privacy of someone who is living there now.

The van showed up on time and took us to the place of assembly. It was a small two-or-three-story building with a little city park next to it. The park had green grass and several benches, around those benches we found a small group of our fellow emigrants and this was where we spent the rest of that day, mostly waiting. First, we were taken into the small office inside the building where we gave the lady sitting there our names and showed our papers. After that, we were instructed to go outside and wait. All communication was in broken Russian, but good enough to understand. Our schedule was not revealed to us, so we just followed the instructions and waited until further notice. The crowd was growing rapidly as more and more families were arriving. When it reached about a hundred or more, the van stopped dumping people and disappeared. In about an hour or so, another van showed up with two men speaking with Israeli accents. They called several names, including our last name, and instructed heads of households to go with them. I and several other guys started walking toward the van. Suddenly we heard a loud argument in the corner of the park between a man and a woman. Then we could see that the man gave up flapping his hand and the woman started walking toward the van. Remember, these were Jewish families from Russia, nothing happens without an argument.

But Israelis took a different approach:

"Madam, are you coming with us?"

"Yes!"

"We just mentioned, only the heads of the households."

"I am the head of the household!"

"Madam, do you have a husband or are you alone?"

"I know him, he will screw everything up! I am going with you!"

"Madam, if you have a husband, he is the head of the household, please step aside."

The poor guy walked with us, I did not wish to be in his shoes at that moment or that night.

A note. I realize, my reader, that in our postmodern society thirty years later this episode may look sexist, but these are the notes of the eyewitnesses, I am just describing the events the way they happened.

The van took us to the Israeli consulate in Vienna. The interview took place in a small room on the second floor, where the Israelis invited us in one at a time. The interviewers were two Israeli men. To my surprise, there was no pressure to convince us to go to Israel at all, I was even a little disappointed. You know, when you are young and ambitious, you think that you are so good, so smart, and so indispensable that everyone wants you and will fight to have you . . . And then you start realizing that no, not really. They do not want you as much as you think, but they might take you, if you ask. That kind of disappointment. This episode was only the beginning, more of those kinds of disappointments were coming.

Anyway, the men asked my name, asked if I was Jewish, and where I was going. I told them that I had a sister in the United States and I hoped to get to San Francisco. The men said OK and at that my interview was over.

After all of us were done with our interviews, the same van delivered us back to the park and the next group was invited. And so on, until the Israelis had a chance to talk to every family. Those families who expressed desire to go to Israel were picked up from the park without delay, grabbed their possessions, and were sent to Israel that same day. There were not that many of them, maybe two or three out of the whole crowd.

The rest of us kept hanging around in the park. In the afternoon they started inviting us for the second interview, this time inside the building, again one family at a time. For some reason, we were not among the first to be called in and waited for several hours. The second interview was with HIAS and Joint (the American Jewish Joint Distribution Committee), two American Jewish charity organizations that were helping Jewish refugees around the world since the beginning of the twentieth century. This interview was with the whole family. Again, names, are any of the family members Jewish, any relatives anywhere in the world, the desired point of destination. At the end of this interview we were instructed to show up the next morning at a certain time and address where we would receive monetary help and further instructions. Then we were released. As we were leaving, we asked how to get to our apartment and were told to take the Metro line, exit at a certain station, and there it would be easy to find.

The problems started at the Metro station. The only money we had with us were U.S. dollars and the station did not accept dollars, only shillings. It was already evening, and all money-exchange shops were closed. Despite being hungry and tired, we had no choice but to walk home. I asked someone for direction, showing the address written in our little green notebook and they waved hands pointing in some direction, which we followed, happy that we wrote down the address. We walked, and walked, and walked along that street. Masha was still OK, Boris became a little cranky, so most of the way I was carrying him. When we hit the railroad tracks, I realized that we need more help. I was looking for someone younger, who was more likely to speak English, but there were very few pedestrians walking by us. Then we spotted a group of young people, two guys and a girl and approached them. They spoke German between themselves, but the girl understood my question in English. She looked in our notebook and shrugged her shoulders, she did not know where it was. Then I asked if she knew the Metro station where we supposed to get out. That was warmer, she said something to her companions, and they started pointing in the direction we were moving but were not sure. It looked like they were not locals, probably tourists themselves. Then the girl's face lit up, like she suddenly remembered something. She walked to the car, parked by the curb about a hundred feet away and walked back with the city map in her hands. We all looked in the map and quickly found the place. Turned out that we indeed were moving in the right direction but had to turn left and follow the tracks until we could cross them and then continue through the streets. I asked them to give me a second and started making a sketch in my notebook not to miss any turn because it was impossible to remember the German names of those streets, but the guys gave us the map, assuring us that they would be OK without it, and that they had another one somewhere, or so we understood. We accepted the gift with great appreciation and cherished it throughout our time in Vienna, then we passed it on to the newly arriving family when we were leaving.

First thing the next morning I went to the currency-exchange place, which happened to be across the street from us, and exchanged twenty bucks for shillings. Then Tatyana and I went to the local small grocery store on the corner and bought our first real food. We were not afraid to leave still-sleeping kids with our little commune. Then we woke up the kids and fed them a real breakfast, not forgetting about ourselves. Our situation had at least started stabilizing.

We found our way to the next assembly place without any trouble—everyone in the dorm already knew how to get there and gave us good directions, plus we had the map. This event was sort of a comforting gathering with Jewish songs I had not heard since my childhood when we visited Korosten, and a few speakers. The message was that we did it, that the worst is behind us, that we should not worry from now on because we will get help, and welcome to freedom. I remember one of the speakers, a woman from Israel who told us that she was originally from Lithuania, that she was not Jewish, that she had lived in Israel for thirty years and loved it and considered it her country. That Israel is a free society, and everyone is welcome there, and so on. For us her message was very comforting because we did not know for sure where we may end up and I was afraid that in Israel we might face backlash discrimination for Tatyana not being Jewish.

A note. To my shame I was underestimating the dignity of my own people. Israel accepted and absorbed tens of thousands of mixed-marriage families, including one of my cousins, and no one was discriminated against. I am talking here about civil rights. Acceptance by religious authorities is a separate story.

At the end of the meeting we received money in shillings and were instructed to come back in a week. I cannot remember exactly how much money we received, but it was enough to sustain our family and even take the kids to the zoo.

Now, when the routines were taken care of, it was time to take care of business. Remember, we had to get rid of three bottles of vodka and two boxes of backgammon, a game that for some reason was in demand in Vienna. Following the instructions from our information sources in the dorm, we went to Vienna's produce market and sold the vodka to a Russian-speaking Israeli merchant, then we went to Vienna's flea market and sold backgammon to the same kind of merchants. We did not get much, but in our situation any money was a blessing.

The week went by quickly. We explored Vienna, went to museums on free-museums day, visited a zoo, and tried pistachio ice cream, best we ever had, as our now-adult children still remember.

One day we met Semion and Lilia and started hanging out together. They had quite a story to tell. The dorm their family was settled in happened to be across the street from a brothel, which was legal in Austria at that time. They had a sixteen-year-old son and a bunch of binoculars and spyglasses for sale in their luggage. To no one's surprise Lilia told us that she caught her boy a couple times looking through the binoculars at the windows across the street. When she complained to Semion, he wisely suggested that there was nothing they could really do about it and that it was better to leave the boy alone. At some point he would probably get bored with it and anyway, how long can you look at those things? Semion's psychological analysis turned out to be correct, and after a few days the kid lost interest.

Another story happened to Semion himself. They had two bottles of French perfume in their luggage that Semion somehow procured in Kishinev and brought with them to sell. After some thoughts, Lilia and he decided that they would probably never find a better place to sell this perfume than that brothel, and Semion went on a mission. With his very limited English, it took the girls some time and confusion to understand what he wanted. When they finally got that he was trying to sell them French perfume, they agreed and offered to pay with their services. We were all cracking up when they told us this story. "I have services across the street in abundance for free," Semoin was laughing, "I need money!" At the end the girls gave him a few bucks and let him go.

We stayed in Vienna for ten days before being transferred to Italy. Historically, the American embassy in Rome was the only place in Europe accepting applications for refugee status, hence every family seeking refuge in the United States was transferred there.

On the morning of departure, a now-familiar van picked up us and our luggage and delivered us to the railroad station. We already knew the drill and just stayed there until the rest of the group arrived. Then the whole group waited for a few more hours until our HIAS escort showed up and instructed us to follow him to the platform. On the platform I noticed men dressed in civilian clothes armed with Uzi machine guns standing in a chain. We understood that they were protecting us from the Arab terrorists. Up to now I have no idea who those men were and what organization hired them, but thanks to them, whoever they were.

Someone may ask me what is the difference between those armed men in Vienna and the armed Russian soldiers in Chop? Why was I so mad there and so appreciative here? Let's start with the position of the men. In Chop they were standing facing us, with their guns pointed at our women and children, hence they were threatening and intimidating us, not protecting. In Vienna they were standing facing outward, their backs turned to us, hence they were protecting us. Plus, they did not point their guns at anyone, the guns were just hanging on their shoulders under their armpits pointed down.

We departed from Vienna that evening and arrived in Rome the next morning. Our group fully occupied three cars of the train. In the middle of the night, when we were crossing the border, the train stopped, and the Italian border patrol walked in accompanied by our HIAS escort. I tried to show them our pieces of paper with typed names, but they ignored me and just counted aloud: uno, due, tre, quattro, then marked something on their sheet and left. In a few minutes our train proceeded. Let me remind you that we never had any Italian visas or any official papers permitting our entry into the country, the feeling was that we really were in the hands of G-d.

When the train started approaching Rome, our guide told us to be ready because we were to get off at a small station before Rome. Was it done for security reasons or out of convenience I do not know. He also told us that the train would stop there only for a few minutes, so we had to make it fast. All of us were already experienced travelers, so we mobilized the men troops again to unload the luggage and let the women take care of the kids. At the station we moved the luggage out of the platform onto the street and after a while an open truck showed up to pick it up, followed by a bus to transport us. The funny episode was when our four-year-old son started crying when the luggage was separated from us: he was already so used to it that it had become part of our family.

The bus took us to a place called, if I am not mistaken, Santa Maria in a little suburban town of Pavona near Rome. The place resembled a resort with a bunch of a little two-story buildings and a large cafeteria/assembly structure in the middle. We were assigned a unit on the second floor with a bathroom. The food was free, three meals a day at the cafeteria. We received some money in

Italian liras and were instructed to find ourselves a place to stay in Rome or a nearby city and to leave the resort within a week. The next money was to be given in two weeks at a certain address in Rome. So, from this point on, our chaperones were taking us off the HIAS teat, now we had to take care of ourselves, except for the money of course.

Next morning all new arrivals were assembled at the Rome central synagogue where the counselors helped us to fill out our applications to the U.S. Department of Justice for refugee status. This is where our first and last names were spelled the way that they are spelled now. On the way there, at the Pavona little railroad station we saw for the first time graffiti "Russi Bastardi," "Palestina Rossa," the swastika, and the red star all next to each other. I guess freedom of speech has its price.

The procedure did not take that long and in the late morning we were already free. At the Termini station while looking for our train to Pavona, I had noticed a train to Nettuno leaving in twenty minutes. The name sounded familiar, I'd heard it in Kiev, somebody's brother was staying there. It meant that if he could find a place to stay in Nettuno, I should be able to too. I even had the name of the street in my green book. The decision was made quickly: Tatyana and the kids were going back to our place in Pavona, I was going straight to Nettuno.

Renting the apartment was not an easy task. Our budget was very limited and finding something in touristy Rome was challenging. Most of our emigrant families were trying to stay in the little coastal towns in close proximity to Rome, where the prices were more reasonable. Our problem was that we came in the middle of summer when those coastal towns were packed with vacationing Romans, which made the available inventory low and the prices high. Another challenge was that we could not rent a whole apartment, even if I found one. We needed to find some partners to share the cost. Italians, we were told, would not negotiate with multiple parties, someone had to enter the contract and then be responsible for the whole gang. My options were either to find an apartment and then find some partners or wait for somebody else's invitation. I decided to try the first option and have the second in reserve. Time was critical, and we decided to make the first move as early as we could.

At the Nettuno railroad station I approached several younger-looking people in hope of engaging them in conversation in English. One woman responded, but the conversation was in Italian anyway. In this regard, Italy was different from Austria, very few people spoke English. When I asked the name of the street that I wrote down in Kiev where I heard someone had rented an apartment, the lady showed me the direction with some explanations, which to my surprise I mostly understood. Italians speak very emotionally using a lots of hand gestures and facial expressions, which makes them easier to understand. Keeping in mind that we Jews from Russia speak in the same manner, made our communication with Italians even easier.

So, I followed the directions, talking to a couple other passersby and learning "bon giorno" and "appartamento" on the way. In about half an hour I found the street, but it did not help me a bit. I approached a middle-aged woman and asked her in English if she knew if someone had an apartment for rent. She showed me with gestures that she did not understand—I could have spoken to her in Russian with the same result. Suddenly her face changed from sorry to a little excited and she asked "Inglese?" I enthusiastically nodded my head. "Uno momento! Uno momento!" she invited me with her gestures to follow her. We walked into a brick-paved courtyard surrounded from all sides by all kinds of buildings of irregular heights, shapes and forms, clustered next to each other, and having glass-covered balconies and air-conditioning units sticking out of the walls and windows, forming a brick and concrete well. I had seen such courtyards before in the south Ukrainian city of Odessa during my business trips. My interlocuteur threw her head back and yelled something in Italian up the well. In a few seconds the well became alive with women showing on the balconies and out of the windows, yelling something back to her. A few minutes later a boy, probably around ten years old, showed up at the courtyard in front of us. "Inglese!" the women pointed at the boy with pride.

I started talking to my interpreter. He studied English in school and knew a few words. I was not a big expert in English, either, but he understood what I wanted and translated it to the woman. She yelled something up the well again and, as I understood, the response was negative. "No" is "No" in any language. This was where I actually heard for the first time the phrase "scusa, adesso no," but did not pay too much attention to it.

After thanking the women and the boy, I continued walking up that same street hoping for a miracle, and a miracle happened! I spotted a young couple and overheard them talking to each other in Russian. This was too much to ask for! The guys gave me the directions to the "House of Joint," which served as a dorm and also as an assembly place for all of the emigrant families settled in the Nettuno area. They suggested that even if I did not find room there, I may at least find some information.

People at the house told me that that morning someone was just looking for renters, that the place is for three families, but that it was too late now, that this person usually comes in the morning. They said that they would tell him that I was interested, and if I came back here tomorrow around 10 a.m., I may find my deal.

I returned back to Pavona late in the evening, told Tatyana what I found, and we started thinking about where to find the two partners that we now needed. She already befriended a next-door family, a woman with two adult children, and suggested that we ask them to join us. The woman's name was Mila, she was in her late forties, with her unmarried son Alek in his mid-twenties, and her younger daughter Lena around eighteen. A very nice family, I actually chatted a minute with Alek that morning at breakfast. The only problem was that they were from Odessa. The legend in our emigrant community was that Italians did not like people from Odessa and would not rent apartments to them. Everyone knew that the Odessits were a little loud and a little too pushy, kind of like New Yorkers are, but no one could understand how the Italians had figured it out so fast? So, taking the Odessits as partners in this endeavor seemed to be risky. But to our credit we did not fall in this trap and decided what the heck, the guys are solid, we will ask them to join us and see what happens.

A note. It turned out, as we learned later, that the phrase "scusa, adesso no" did not mean that they did not want to take people from Odessa, but was simply translated as "sorry, not now." A perfect example of how a lack of knowledge or simple misinterpretation could turn into perceived prejudice.

Mila and Alek happily accepted our offer to join forces. Alek was actually planning to go and start looking for apartments himself the next morning but did not know where to start. Now we needed a third partner. Mila suggested a young couple without children from Mogillev, Belorussia, she met that day. We went to their room and offered them to join us. To my surprise they were a little hesitant and started asking how we were going to split the money? We said three ways, three rooms—three equal parts. They suggested that we should split it proportional to the number of people. That made no difference for Mila and Alek, but our family had to pay twice more than they did, despite me finding the apartment. I disagreed, and Alek supported me. Nobody forced them, they could stay out of the deal, we would find someone else. After some thought they agreed and we decided that the next day, first thing in the morning, three men would go to Nettuno and get that deal.

The "apartment" we rented was in reality a furniture warehouse, which a local furniture merchant, Signor Paladini, being a good businessman, quickly remodeled into apartments. A long barrack was divided into two equal sections, mirroring each other and separated by a wall. Each section had a big window and a door.

Walking into the door, which was on the right end of the section, there was a common area in front and three compartments in the back, separated by the walls, but open-faced without doors. Kind of like stalls in public restrooms, but with partitions up to the ceiling. In the common area there was a big table next to the window, with chairs. In the left front corner was a restroom and a shower compartment. The restroom had a door—thank you Signor, Paladini! In the far-left corner was a sink and a stove. Each bedroom compartment had two bunk beds, hence sleeping four. In front of the barrack there was a big yard with lounge chairs. I was the responsible party, signing the contract for one section. The other section was not occupied yet when we were renting ours, but three other families from our Pavona place took it as soon as we returned back and told people that it was available. So, a total of six families ended up living in our barrack. When our women saw what we had rented, we received a lot of "compliments," but we got a place to stay, the Mediterranean beach was a twenty-minute walk away, and the price was reasonable. The furniture office was on the other side of the fence and Signor Paladini did not mind if we used his office phone for incoming calls from Russia and Ukraine, his secretary would just yell, "Telefonare!" and the nearest of us would run to the office and figure out who was the receiving party.

Besides our new friends from Odessa, we befriend two other families. One of them was a single woman Anya, from Kharkov, with two teenage sons, Slava and Eugene. Another was also a single woman, Lilia from Kiev, with two daughters in their twenties. Her older girl had some sort of mental deviation and was handicapped.

We happily lived in this place for two months. A little risqué detail: All the single women in our group later confessed that each of them at some point received a dirty proposition from Signor Paladini, but he never approached young girls or married women.

Trying to Prove the Obvious

We spent almost four months in Italy. Our hope was to receive permission to enter the United States as refugees. To receive such permission, we had to apply to the United States Immigration and Naturalization Service (INS), the agency of the U.S. Department of Justice, located at the American embassy in Rome, and have an interview with the INS officials. The purpose of the interview was to convince the officials that we were persecuted in the country of our origin or are afraid of being persecuted if we return. Fair and simple. Our Jewish refugees' relief agency HIAS was helping us with the applications and counseling.

The problem was that at the time we were applying, about 70 to 80% of the applicants were receiving denials. These families were called "refuseniks." They kept staying in Italy, accumulating in numbers, and trying to appeal. Some of them were old Soviet refuseniks, hanging out in Italy for a year and longer. All of us were a carbon copy of each other, Jewish or mixed families, fed up with being people of second grade, stripped of our citizenship by the country of our origin. What criteria the INS was using in selecting which family was accepted and which was denied, was a mystery. It certainly was not about percentage of Jewish blood, it was not the region of the country, it was not a person's occupation or education. The composition of the family, the presence of elderly or children did not matter. There were a few mathematicians in the crowd who were trying to collect the incoming information and create an algorithm. They also failed to figure it out. By all observations it looked like a random pick. Looking back at it after living in the U.S. for almost thirty years, however, now I have a slightly different opinion, which I will share later. I have to admit that single mothers and families with handicapped members were practically guaranteed to be accepted. Taking this into account, the percentage of denials was even higher.

So, after filling out applications at the Rome synagogue on the second day after our arrival, we started waiting for our interview in the American embassy. The process took about three to four weeks. Ahead of the interview we had a meeting with our HIAS counselor, a young, red-haired, American man about my age. The guy spoke decent Russian. He started with asking us why we decided to leave the Soviet Union. Tatyana and I tried to tell our story, explaining how difficult it was to get an education, to find a decent job, to live under constant anti-Semitic pressure from the authorities and from the surrounding environment. His reaction was shocking to us. He gave us a long tirade, telling that he was once in Vladivostok, that he liked it so much, and that we just did not understand what we were doing and how beautiful it was out there. In other words, in his eyes we were running away from paradise. It looked to me like the guy was a devout Communist. I am not sure what was he doing there. Maybe he took the job trying to understand why people would run away from what he considered to be a solution to all American problems? But I am pretty sure that he did not learn anything because he was not listening and the whole session was spent trying to convince us that we were wrong. Anyway, our conversation could have been an interesting exchange of opinions, but the value of help from our counselor, who was supposed to prepare us for the interview, was next to zero.

All our communication with HIAS, all schedules, and all appointments were through the Joint House. Every evening all our little community gathered on the street in front of the house. Whole families with kids were coming from all corners of Nettuno and surrounding little towns. Around 7 p.m. a couple of our guys, not sure if they were volunteers or were hired by HIAS, would come out with a bunch of paperwork in their hands and make their announcements yelling into the crowd. Everything was open and public, right there on the square, the way it could have probably happened in Ancient Greece, at least in my imagination. The men would first call the last name. If a person was present, they'd announce if the family was scheduled for the counseling meeting, for the interview, or was approved or was denied. The latter list was growing every day. After each announcement, they'd hand out the corresponding letter from HIAS.

Meanwhile, every two weeks I was making my trips to Rome to receive the assistance money for our family. This duty was solely on me. The place was somewhere deep inside the city, and the lines were huge. I usually took the first train from Nettuno to Rome, and then the bus from Termini Station to the place. On my second trip there, I decided to walk back instead of taking the bus, as I was in no hurry. I figured out the general direction from where the bus was coming and just followed my instincts. I've been to unfamiliar cities many times before, so I was not afraid to get lost. I walked and walked, enjoying new sights, when suddenly a huge wall, right in front of me, was blocking my way. The wall was as far as I could see both to my right and to my left. I decided to go left, around my new obstacle, trying to understand on my way what it was. After about an hour of walking along the wall, I came to a beautiful plaza that I recognized from photos and postcards I had seen. The wall surrounded the city of the Vatican and the plaza was St. Peter's Square.

Staying at the square I remembered that somebody at our evening gatherings told me that you can get a newspaper printed in Russian at the Vatican. I walked around the plaza and did not find anything. I asked at the newsstand—nothing. I started thinking maybe inside the Vatican? Though I had big doubts, I started walking a little away from St. Peter's Square, until I saw a gate and a Swiss Guard in a very colorful and beautiful uniform at the gate. I asked him if he spoke English and received a "Yes." Then I tried to explain to him what I was looking for. When I heard him answering, I realized that this guy really spoke English and me, not so much. His English was perfect. The guard very politely told me that he did not know where to get a Russian newspaper but could assure me with all his confidence that it would not be inside the Vatican City. Then he suggested I look in the block next to the square where there were some stores and wished me good luck. I walked to that block and found what I was looking for. It was a small grocery and convenience store run by Russian emigrants from the old times. Now we have quite a few similar stores run by the new wave of immigrants in San Francisco. In this store they were giving away a free Russian-language newspaper, issued by the old Russian emigrant community in Paris. I grabbed a newspaper and happily went home, reading it on the train. Remember, in previous chapters I had mentioned the "Whites" and the "Reds" in the Russian Civil War in the early '20s? This newspaper was issued by the leftovers of the "Whites." For our generation these people were shrouded in mystery and even some romanticism. Even the official Soviet propaganda had lately switched from portraying them as a pure evil enemy to people who "just made a mistake." Now we were making the same "mistake," and it was intriguing to peek into these people's world.

A note. Later I met a few of those guys in San Francisco. One of them, Irene, a daughter of those emigrants born in the United States, was my coworker for ten years and a good friend; unfortunately, she has passed away from illness. Aside from the religious beliefs, I have not noticed any difference between them and us. Their Russian sounded a little funny, though. Generally, both groups carry the same culture, maybe with slightly different spice.

The other business we had to take care of was selling our merchandise, which consisted of one photo camera, a few opera glasses, a couple of spyglasses, several hand watches, and a few amber necklaces. All selling actions took place at a local Nettuno market twice a week on the town's main street. The market was mostly produce, but there were a few local stands with sunglasses and some other touristy items. We usually stood along the market street displaying our items on our arms, or just walked with the crowd offering our items. This is where most of the conversational Italian was picked up very quickly. The only obstacle to our business was local police, in sight of which we had to hide our merchandise because we, of course, did not have sales licenses. The police never arrested anyone, just confiscated the merchandise from the unfortunates they caught. A pity, but not catastrophic. To cope with this, we tried not to have more than one or two items on hand at a time.

The free time was spent on the beautiful Nettuno beach, studying the *National Electrical Code Handbook*, my treasure I brought from our trip to America. I cannot say that I learned much there, but at least I was making an effort.

In a few weeks at the evening gathering we received a letter with the invitation for our interview. I do not remember now the date and time. We were all invited together, Tatyana and I, and both of our children—they wanted to see everyone. There were two interviewers from INS, a man and a woman, and an interpreter. They were asking questions, we were giving answers, there was no storytelling. I was nervous. As I had explained earlier, we were poorly prepared. In addition to a very weak counselor, there was a cultural abyss between our interviewers and us. In our minds, if we could only show to our interviewers that our intentions were to go to America to work hard, that we had an education and occupation that was in demand, that we were qualified workers, that we would be able to sustain ourselves and would not be a burden to our new country, why would they turn us away and deny us?

In their eyes we looked like typical white Europeans, educated and self-sustainable, that do not fit a refugee profile. Trying to prove that we were persecuted and discriminated against in our country of origin was practically impossible in this environment.

So, you are telling us that you were not accepted to colleges, but you have a college degree, are you not? You are telling us that you were discriminated against at the workplaces, but you were not unemployed, were you not? You are telling us that you were persecuted, but you have no criminal record . . . And so on.

How can you prove in this kind of an interview that the college you were accepted to was not the college you were qualified for and that the occupation you studied was not what you wanted to do, that you were accepted only because of a low enrollment in that college for that occupation, that you worked for ridiculously low wages practically as a slave laborer? How can you and why should you prove anything, standing in front of them in this foreign country without any paperwork, stripped off your born citizenship? Sometimes it is very difficult to prove the obvious!

The questions continued, but I started having feelings that something was going wrong. If we only knew back then what we know now, our answers would be more personal, with examples, with more complaints, with tears and pity. But we kept ourselves open and honest and this turned out to become our problem.

I was listening to their questions very carefully, trying to understand the question in its original language, and then waited for the interpreter to receive confirmation that I understood it correctly before answering. The English part I understood maybe 10%, at best. But at some point, toward the end of the interview, there came a very simple question that I completely understood, and I started answering right away, without waiting for the interpreter. Both of our interviewers looked at each other with surprise:

"Do you speak English?

"Yes, a little, I studied it at school."

Their faces looked disturbed, like I'd hidden something from them. Maybe they were saying something to each other that I was not supposed to hear? I do not know, I did not understand that well. If it bothered them that much, they could have asked me in the beginning . . . Anyway, after this little episode the interview was quickly over, and we were told that we would be informed about their decision by mail.

A few more weeks passed. Every evening we were in front of the Joint House waiting to know our fate. We still hoped for the better. Maybe we misinterpreted the expressions of their faces? By our logic, understanding English should have been considered an advantage, should it not? But one of the evenings we had heard our names called. Unfortunately, we joined the lengthy list of "refusniks." We still have this note from HIAS dated August 3rd, 1989.

After the denial, HIAS had automatically placed our applications for appeal—thank you, HIAS. But the process was lengthy and had even less chances of success. It was already August, the nights were becoming colder, Paladini's barracks did not have heat, so it was time to think about a new place. Our friend Mila, being a single mother, was approved, and they were waiting for the departure. The other young couple from Mogilev was also denied and they wanted to move out. Our group started falling apart.

At that time, I had already picked up a little bit of a conversational Italian and decided to try my luck using these new skills. I walked up the shore a few blocks from the Joint House where there were nice, two-story, multi-unit townhouses with little front yards and balconies and started asking if anyone would rent us an apartment. At the end of August the situation changed from that in the mid-summer when I was looking for our first place. The vacationing city dwellers started leaving the town and demand for rentals became much lower. In one of the units a young woman, whose name was Maria, told me that her neighbor Lucia may be interested and that I should come back in the evening. The most amazing thing was that Maria did not speak a word of English, all conversation was in Italian, but miraculously we understood each other.

In the evening I came with Tatyana and we met Lucia. She showed us the place and we agreed on the price, but her condition was that I first had to talk to her husband who spoke English and would be there in a few days for the weekend. I came back over the weekend and met her husband. The guy was working for Siemens and did speak English, which made our conversation much, much easier and productive. The husband, unfortunately I do not remember his name, explained to me that this was their summer residence and that he did not mind renting it to us, but was not very comfortable with a verbal agreement and would like to register it with the police. Polite and very logical in our situation— cannot blame him, I'd do the same.

On our way to the police station I started thinking about what I could show them as my ID? A typed piece of paper with Russian text and

Czechoslovakian, Austrian, and Israeli visa stamps? There was no Italian visa stamp there! On the other hand, I was thinking, the police knew very well that we were here, in their town, they were shooing us at the marketplace after all. So, I decided to relax and see what happened.

At the police station the officer did not even want to look at my piece of paper, he just gave me a form to fill out. The form was of course in Italian, so my landlord had to translate it to me line by line. The part with the names was easy, but when it came to the place of permanent residence, I was not sure what to fill. I explained to my host that at the moment we do not have a permanent residence and offered to write my sister's address in the United States, that this was at least the place where we were heading. The policemen shook his head, no, the place you came from. You should have come from somewhere? I did not argue, just wrote our old Kiev address and we both signed the deal.

The place was perfect! A big living room with a kitchen and a restroom downstairs and two bedrooms, a restroom with shower, and a balcony upstairs. The living room had a TV, which we had not watched since Kiev! Never mind that all programs were in Italian, it just sharpened our skills. But the biggest treasure was a washing machine in the downstairs bathroom! The era of hand-washing our clothes was finally over! The price was a little higher than Paladini's barracks, but we could afford it. All communications and payments went through Maria, who lived next door with her family. Maria was a very nice and friendly lady, and she and Tatyana quickly became friends and were often chatting about their women's affairs, miraculously understanding each other. Maria did not mind if we used her phone for incoming calls, so we could talk to our parents. We did not abuse her hospitality too much and most often used the Nettuno central post office for our calls, but sometimes our parents used her number.

Once Tatyana's parents mixed the time difference and called very early, around 6 a.m. We woke up to screams of "Signora! Telefono! Telefono!" coming from the street. We jumped up and ran out to the balcony. Downstairs there was Maria in her nightgown in the middle of the street waving to us with her hands. Tatyana ran down and both ladies in their nightgowns and bare feet started running along the street toward Maria's unit. It looked like a scene from a Fellini movie. Only in Italy!

Actually, after our deal went through, many other Italians in this complex started renting their units to Russian emigrant families—I guess we passed the OK test.

A note. Up to this time our family still has a good sentimental feeling toward Italy and Italians. This was the country that gave us our first refuge without even looking into our paperwork, and these were the people who made us feel welcome, allowing us to blend in and live among them for as long as we needed. As a small tribute, when we go to the store to buy something and see "Made in Italy" on the label, we buy it even if it is more expensive. I am not talking about a Ferrari and Maserati, of course.

In time all of our stuff was sold, so we would only go to the marketplace to buy our food. By the way, when we started receiving our assistance money, we understood that it was coming from the Jewish charities. In the Soviet Union there was no such thing as kosher food, the concept of it just did not exist. We ate what we could find and there was no marking or list of ingredients on the package. But now the situation changed. So, our family, Tatyana, the kids, and I, had a meeting and decided that it would be swinishness to buy pork using this money and completely excluded pork, shrimp, and other traditionally non-Jewish food items from our ration.

Every two weeks I continued going to Rome to receive our assistance money. Our status in Italy did not allow us to work, and we were warned about it clearly and strongly. The sea became cold and beach time was over. We had nothing better left to do but wait.

Our big concern was that Masha was missing school and we did not know how long our situation might last. Sending a twelve-year-old girl to a new school just for a few months in a foreign country with the foreign language and a foreign culture? We felt uneasy about this and decided to wait a little while longer.

More and more people continued arriving and more and more families were receiving the denials. There was a joke circulating in our emigrant community at that time about two guys meeting on the street of one of those coastal Italian towns, one having just received permission, and the other receiving a denial. So, the one who received the denial asked:

"Listen, what did you tell them in the interview that they gave you permission?"

"Well, I told them a story about how they tortured me at the KGB."

"Interesting, I told them the same. What exactly?"

"I told them that the KGB agents took a crowbar, made it red-hot in the fireplace and stuck it up my ass!"

"Amazing! I told them exactly the same story!"

"With the cold end in."

"???"

"So that you would burn your hands trying to pull it out."

In the evenings at the Joint House we would all gather together and discuss our situations. Many had relatives in the United States, many of them in New York, and some of them with connections in the American Jewish community. Our case became known. There were tens of thousands of us accumulating in and around Rome, and we started attracting attention. At some point some of our guys started receiving suggestions from their sources in the United States that we should become more visible, make some noise, attract the press to make our case better known. Otherwise, if we remained silent, nobody was going to do anything. So, people started becoming organized, not only in Nettuno, but across the whole Rome region where our emigrants were settled. This brought out some natural leaders, who started to represent our little community. These leaders organized a rally in Rome in front of the American embassy. I was not among the leaders, but I was a participant. Our rally did not request anything, we were very careful about this. We were only asking the question "Why?" Why America had fought for our freedom for so many years and now did not want to take us? Why did we have to prove the obvious? Why this random selection? If there is a limited number you can accept, tell us, we will wait in line! But at least give us some explanation of what is going on!

The rally was pretty big, a few thousand people. The media was there, I believe CNN and some others—I cannot recall if it was ABC or NBC. We signed a petition to the U.S. Congress, and listened to a few speakers, who to my surprise showed up at our rally. Some of them were elected officials from the United States. One speaker was a representative from the Italian Jewish community, who told us that if America continued refusing us, he would apply to Italian government on our behalf for help. This was very nice of him. Should things have turned that way, this story would have been written in Italian. At the end of the rally the American ambassador came to us and told us that he would pass our message on.

Our case indeed became known in the United States and the U.S. Congress approved an amendment, introduced by the U.S. Senator from New Jersey, Frank Lautenberg, which allowed certain groups from the Soviet Union, i.e. Jews, Evangelical Christians, and Ukrainian Catholics, to be eligible for refugee status without having proved individual persecution or fear of persecution. In other words, this amendment recognized that certain groups in the Soviet Union were persecuted by default and, if the applicant could prove that he or she belonged to such a group, the applicant did not need to prove that he or she was persecuted individually. Exactly our case.

The amendment also had a provision for families like ours, who were earlier denied refugee status. We were paroled into the United States on a humanitarian basis and, after acquiring one year of physical presence in the

United States, were allowed to apply for lawful permanent resident status, also known as a "green card."

The Lautenberg Amendment became Public Law 101-167 in November 1989. This law moved the place for accepting applications for refugee status from Rome to the United States Embassy in Moscow, therefore closing the historical Italian route.

As far as our family is concerned, we received a letter dated October 10, 1989, from the District Director of the Department of Justice that, pursuant to the United States Attorney General's directive of September 14, 1989, our application had been reopened, reviewed and approved. And then it was followed by the list of sections and paragraphs under which our application had been approved. Italy started being cleaned up. We were among the first group of Italian refuseniks sent to the United States, at least from Nettuno.

We were instructed to be ready and stand with our luggage in front of the Joint House on November 3rd at 9 p.m. This time it was not a van, but a big comfortable bus that took us to the Fiumicino—Aeroporto Internazionale Leonardo da Vinci. Our flight to New York was early in the morning, but HIAS did not take any chances and delivered us the night before. Waiting was our second occupation by then, so we patiently waited overnight and finally boarded the plane.

A note. The cost of tickets from Rome to San Francisco we later paid back to HIAS. This was the only money we were asked to pay back because the tickets were expensive, and it would allow HIAS to help other refugees. Of course, we have been giving some donations to the Jewish community every year ever since.

We landed in New York's JFK on November 4, 1989, this date is remembered in our family every year and I hope will be remembered in the future. At the airport the INS officer gave each of us an I-94 form, which was again a piece of paper, 4 inches by 4.5 inches, with handwritten Family Name, First Name, Birth Date, and Country of Citizenship for some reason marked as "USSR." The form did not have any photo, but it had a stamp that said, "Admitted as a refugee," and the most important part: "Employment Authorized."

When Tatyana and I walked into the airport hall, both of us instantly recognized the smell. It was a very distinct sweet smell of bubblegum mixed with some other spices, maybe coffee. For us it was the sweet smell of America. We looked at each other and hugged. Yes, our journey was over, we were finally home. From now on everything was gonna be OK!

A few months after our arrival, in distant 1990, Tatyana and I were standing in our local Safeway store discussing something in our native tongue. A woman came up to us and asked what language we were speaking. When she found that we were Russians, she asked if we were Jewish, by any chance. We responded that yes, we are.

Then she asked:

"Listen, they were collecting money for you at our synagogue, and we gave some. Can you tell me, were they really helping you?"

And we responded:

"Yes, ma'am, they helped us and sustained our family all the way through. Thank you, ma'am!"

Epilogue

W e have now lived in the United States for almost thirty years. The adaptation process went fairly easy and in 1995 we became Americans. I worked in different places from a maintenance electrician at the paint manufacturing factory to a project manager in one of the prominent San Francisco engineering consulting firms, took part in countless start-ups of electric power distribution and generation substations throughout California, Arizona, and Nevada, from deserts in the south to mountains in the north. I could write another book about how we did it and about the wonderful people I met on my way. Tatyana fell in love with computers and was working for many years as a software engineer in big-name Silicon Valley hi-tech companies.

My father came to United States one year after us in, 1991, sponsored by my sister. In 1996, after we became U.S. citizens, we sponsored Tatyana's parents and brought them in. All of them are still with us.

We gave our children a so-desired college education. More than that, when I got my first management position and realized that my college course of "political economy of socialism" was not much help in the market-driven economy, I enrolled in university myself and received my MBA. It was not free, but it was open to all without nationality quotas.

I learned more about Jewish history and Jewish traditions. I learned, for example, that every Jewish male in every generation for about four thousand years back to Avraham went through the ritual of brit milah (circumcision) regardless of the circumstances that generation lived in at that time. Learning this, I realized that this chain of generations was broken on me. I, my generation, was the link that had been cut through! How could I let Nazis and Commies have this victory, let them leave this scar on the face of the Earth before being flushed down into the drain of history?! So, we convinced a Hassidic rabbi to perform this ritual on me and my son. I was 41, Boris was 12. Physically it was an insignificant outpatient medical procedure, I drove us back home that day twenty miles from the medical office in my stick-shift-operated truck and went back to work the next Monday. But spiritually it was our Victory Day. That day we overcame all evil efforts of our villains and haters to destroy our people and repaired the chain! Both of my grandsons had their brit on the seventh day, as prescribed by Jewish tradition. Now it's up to them.

We traveled around the world but have never been back either to Russia or to Ukraine. Not because we cannot or are afraid to, it's just . . . too hard emotionally. I cannot say how they are treating their minorities now, I do not live there. All I know is that neither of these countries ever considered correcting the historic injustice and restoring our birthright citizenship. Not that we need it. I think they need it more than us for their own records.

I know that some people in the Soviet Union and now in Russia still consider us to be "the betrayers of the motherland." To them I can say that Soviet Union never was our mother. It was rather a mean and vicious stepmother who hated her own children and tolerated her stepchildren to the extent of "just be thankful that I left you alive."

America, on the other hand, resembles to me a wise and loving foster mother who loves her children so much that she would never allow her biological children to have any advantages over her adopted children, which makes them all stronger, mutually respectful, united, and loving of their Mom. America accepted us as equals, from the first moment we stepped onto her soil with those 4-inch by 4.5-inch pieces of paper in our hands. Of course, it was difficult; of course, at the beginning we were doing less-qualified jobs. But it was not because we were Jewish, or Russians, or anything else. It was because we still had to learn English and acquire necessary skills. Fair, simple, and open. This is why when our family, Russian-born, Ukraine-born, and American-born, pilgrims and immigrants with their American spouses and first-generation American kids, gather together around the Thanksgiving table, our first toast is always G-d Bless America!

The United States of America is an amazing experiment in the history of humankind. We are proudly participating in this experiment as citizens and sincerely want it to succeed. The Soviet Union was also an amazing experiment, subjugating a quarter-billion population in an artificially created informational vacuum for seventy-four years. As survivors of that experiment, we do not want humankind to forget the results.

In conclusion, a few words to the first-generation Americans of every background who happen to read this book and to those generations that follow. The pursuit of happiness without liberty is nonsense. When we realized this self-evident truth, we, the modern-day pilgrims, did everything we could for you to be born free. The task was not easy, but it was simple and clear. I hope that you will be able to manage a much more complex and challenging task of remaining free.

www.ingramcontent.com/pod-product-compliance
Lightning Source LLC
LaVergne TN
LVHW051255080426
835509LV00020B/2984